BACCHUS AT BAKER STREET

Observations on the Bibulous Preferences of Mr. Sherlock Holmes and his Contemporaries

Patricia Guy

IAN HENRY PUBLICATIONS

© Patricia Guy, 1995

ISBN 0 86025 286 8

Library of Congress Cataloging-in-Publication Data

Guy, Patricia
    Bacchus at Baker Street : observations on the bibulous preferences of Mr Sherlock Holmes and his contemporaries / by Patricia Guy.
        p.   cm.
    Includes bibliographical references (p.)
    ISBN 0-88734-917-X
    1. Doyle, Arthur Conan, Sir, 1859-1930--Characters--Sherlock Holmes. 2. Alcoholic beverages in literature. 3. Holmes, Sherlock (Fictitious character). 4. Alcoholic beverages--Great Britain--History--19th century. 5. Detective and mystery stories, English-History and criticism. 6. Private investigators in literature. 7. Drinking behaviour in literature. I. Title.
PR4624.G89 1995
823'.8--dc20   95-14831

Printed by
Watkiss Studios Ltd.
Holme Court, Biggleswade, Bedfordshire SG18 9ST
for
Ian Henry Publications, Ltd.
20 Park Drive, Romford, Essex RM1 4LH

DEDICATION

The book is dedicated to Dr. J. H. Watson for the kindness he has shown me over the years.

O! there is nothing like fine weather, and health, and books, and a fine country, and a contented mind, and a diligent habit of reading, and thinking, and an amulet against ennui - and, please heaven, a little Claret cool out of cellar a mile deep - with a few or a good many ratafia cakes - a rocky basin to bathe in, a strawberry bed to say your prayers to flora in, a pad nag to go you ten miles or so; two or three spiteful folks to spar with; two or three odd fishes to laugh at andf two or three numskulls to argue with - instead of using dumb bells on a rainy day.

John Keats
From a letter to Fanny Keats: 1st May, 1819

Give her a bottle of beer, a novel and a nice fire,
and that's all she wants.
From the Metropolitan Police Courts
3rd March, 1929

Contents

Acknowledgements	1
Wines, spirits and their accoutrements in crime and the art of detection	3
The cultural and vinicultural milieu of Mr. Sherlock Holmes	9
A case of identity: the essence of Tokay	15
Shall I open a flask?: the cellar of Mr Thaddeus Sholto	23
Ancient and cobwebby bottles	27
A comet year	35
Vintage charts: claret; red burgundy; white burgundy; champagne; port	37
Copitas and robbers: diverting trifles regarding the wines of Jerez	49
Consumer dourobles: a study of Victorian port styles	55
The curious case of the caged cork: sparkling effusions in the Methode Champenoise	59
Yea! Pure wine of the grape: the Utahlitarian approach to winemaking	65
The tantalus: whisky and brandy	69
The sprit case: gin; rum; curaçoa	75
Behind bars: Victorian mixed drinks	79
A study in claret: what drives a wine merchant to crime?	93
What was in the cellar besides Mrs Toller?	97
His last glass: remedies for rheumatism	101
What the doctor ordered: Victorian medical imbibing	105
The science of degustation	115
Medicinal brews	123
Bibliography	133

ACKNOWLEDGEMENTS

Verona is a wonderful place to live - the opera; the piazze, the luscious, swirling autumn fog - but the library system here is as impenetrable as the A.C. Milan defence and it is very difficult to wait for my yearly trips to London and New York.

I should, therefore, like to thank my friends for their amusing letters and their research on my behalf. Allow me, dear readers, to name names: Joan Walker, Rita Scribner, Richard Hudd, Russell Atwood, Thom Utecht, James Fletcher, Evelyn Herzog, Susan Griswold, Lucy Zawadski, Mary Ellen Rich, Francine Swift, Pat Moran, Katie Powell, Dore Nash, Maggie McNie, MW., and Shirley Purvis. Thanks to Bill Vander Water for sending a steady supply of English-language detective novels.

Thanks are also due to Daniel Block for allowing me to borrow from his superb collection of English-language wine books and to Annalisa Morandini for access to the books in her library.

I am also grateful to Guinness Archivist, Peter Walsh, for sending me photocopies of unpublished correspondence and to Allegra Antinori for sending facsimiles of her grandfather's letters; to Giles MacDonogh and Stephen Brook for their Tokay-inspired reminiscences; to Matthew Gloag of Matthew Gloag & Son for his superb toddy recipe; to the Gin & Vodka Association of Great Britain, The Scotch Whisky Association, Comité Interprofessionnel du Vin de Champagne, The Church of the Latter-day Saints, and the Navoo Historical Society for their tireless research; to Michael Broadbent for answering my many queries about older vintages and to Serena Sutcliffe for sending information on auction prices. The companies of de Kuyper, Bols, Beefeater, Harveys of Bristol, International Distillers & Vintners Limited, and Irish Distillers Limited all very kindly sent me information.

A Very Special thanks to Michael Benson for his witty and concise criticism and his way with foreign phrases.

And thanks to the ever faithful Edmund Cane for being ever faithful.

WINES, SPIRITS, AND THEIR ACCOUTREMENTS IN CRIME AND THE ART OF DEDUCTION

> All knowledge comes useful
> to the detective.
> Mr. Sherlock Holmes
> *The Valley of Fear*

Drawing by Frank Wiles for *The Valley of Fear*

The solutions to many of the Great Detective's most difficult cases hinge upon his familiarity with libations and the habits of imbibers. The untouched whisky, the ravaged cork, the scratches around the keyhole, all provide the keen eye of Mr. Sherlock Holmes with important clues in his search for the truth.

He locates the mysterious FHM, retrieves an errant heiress and foils the plans of a lordly suitor all by understanding the quality/price ratio of fine wines. As the following exchange between himself and Dr. Watson taken from *The Adventure of the Noble Bachelor* illustrates.

"...friend Lestrade held information in his hands the value of which he did not himself know. The initials were, of course, of the highest importance, but more valuable still was it to known that within a week he had settled his bill at one of the most select London hotels.

"And how did you deduce the select?"

"...eightpence for a glass of sherry pointed to one of the most expensive hotels. There are not many in London which charge at that rate."

In the midst of an investigation, Mr. Holmes often seeks the convivial atmosphere of a local tavern and he encourages Doctor Watson to do the same. "Go to the nearest public house," he advises his friend. "That is the centre of country gossip." This proves so time and again. The benevolent host of the Green Dragon Tavern, Mr. Josiah Barnes, puts Mr. Holmes on the scent in *The Adventure of Shoscombe Old Place*; thoughtful Mr. Windigate, landlord of the Alpha Inn, points Mr. Holmes towards the thief of the Blue Carbuncle; and the unnamed but no less loquacious landlord of the pub near Chiltern Grange helps bring a happy ending to *The Adventure of the Solitary Cyclist*.

The hosts of two conveniently placed inns provide important data in *The Adventure of Priory School*. The illness of the Red Bull's landlady keep people alert all through the night of young Lord Saltire's abduction and the unsuitable manner of Mr. Reuben Hayes, landlord of the squalid Fighting Cock Inn, arouses the detective's suspicions.

Mr. Holmes appreciates the camaraderie that sharing a jar of half and half or a bumper of wine creates, as this extract from *The Adventure of Shoscombe Old Place* demonstrates:

"Meanwhile, if we mean to keep up our characters. I suggest we have our host in for a glass of his own wine and hold some high converse upon eels and dace, which seems to be the straight road to his affections. We may chance upon some useful gossip in the process."

This keen student of humankind soon grasped the relationship between one's tipple of choice and one's identity, character and occupation. In *The Adventure of Black Peter* this understanding exonerates one fellow - "Do you think the anaemic youth... was the man who hobnobbed in rum and water with Black Peter in the dead of night?" - and lays guilt at the doorstep of another, much to the awestruck admiration of Mr. Stanley Hopkins.

"Mr. Holmes," said Hopkins, "Even now I do not understand how you attained this result."

"Simply by having the good fortune to get the right clue from the beginning.... The amazing strength... the rum and water... all pointed to a seaman..."

Drunks often become unintentional accomplices. In some cases for the good, as when Mr. Toller, stupefied on drink, leaves the way clear for Miss Alice's escape from Copper Beeches (whilst a strongly fortified wine-cellar detains Mrs. Toller).

Others participate in their own demise, as when Black Peter's horrific cry as the harpoon pierces his body is taken for his usual drunken roar and when in *A Study in Scarlet*, Mr. Enoch Drebber's insobriety makes him easy prey for Jefferson Hope's murderous revenge.

The canny Mr. Hope, then, escapes from Constable John Rance by performing a hammy, but none the less effective, interpretation of a street-corner toper.

"I've seen many a drunk chap in my time," [Rance] said, "but never anyone so cryin' drunk as that cove. He was at the gate when I came out, a'leanin' up ag'in the railings, and a'singin' at the pitch o' his lungs about Columbine's New-fangled Banner, or some such stuff. He couldn't stand, far less help."

"I'm afraid, Rance, that you will never rise in the force," Holmes replies dryly. Had Rance but spent a bit more time at the White Hart Inn studying the finer points of drunken comportment he might have won his sergeant's stripes that night.

The popular notion that brandy restores flagging health allows clever wrong-doers to take advantage of the instinctive response of the good samaritan. In *The Adventure of The Three Students*, for example, the faithful Bannister collapses on vital evidence and is left to sip a revivifying brandy until such time as he can remove the damning items. Lady Hilda, in *The Adventure of the Second Stain*, feigns a faint that sends the constable on the trot to the Ivy Plant for a tonic tot. During his absence she deftly removes hidden documents.

Mr. Holmes depends heavily upon his vinous knowledge when he visits Abbey Grange. The victim, Sir Eustace, is a bellowing beast when he is under the influence, and wine and vinous paraphernalia -

decanter, cork, wine bottle and glasses - provides vital clues.

When Mr. Stanley Hopkins concludes the villains must have been in league with one of the servants; he is left to ponder which of them it might be?

"All things being equal," said Holmes, "one would suspect the one at whose head the master threw a decanter."

The villains, it appears, have refreshed themselves with a bottle of Sir Eustace's wine. The long deeply coloured cork - a clue in itself that the wine is of high quality - has been marred by a screw not over an inch and a half long, proving that the corkscrew kept in the dinning room had not been used. Mr. Holmes concludes that one of the culprits 'will have one of those multi-knives'. Could there be a more telling clue to a chap's character?

Then there is the sticky problem of those three wine glasses so conveniently left by the intruders. To Mr. Hopkins this suggest that three thirst-quenched robbers are now at large. Mr. Holmes is not convinced. To him presence of beeswing in one of the glasses indicates "that only two glasses were used, and the dregs of both were poured into a third glass, so as to give the false impression that three people had been here. In that way all the beeswing would be in the last glass, would it not?"

The presence of beeswing further indicates that the wine was a fine old Port. Mr. C. W. Berry, tells us beeswing "is the final effort of the formation of a good crust, which in itself does not contain the density of an ordinary crust... Unless you looked for it you would not notice it and connoisseurs consider it an added charm in suspense."

Mr. Hopkins's theory that the crime was perpetrated by a gang of professional burglars is refuted by Mr. Holmes, who muses: "...I should say, that it was most unusual for such men to leave a bottle half empty."

This observation, as with other of the Great Detective's insights into the behaviour of his fellow man, is based on experience that could only be gleaned 'down the pub'. Is it not logical to suggest that some of Mr. Holmes's long absences from his flat in Baker Street may have been spent lifting a pint at his cosy neighbourhood local?

Drawing by Sydney Paget for *The Adventure of the Abbey Grange*

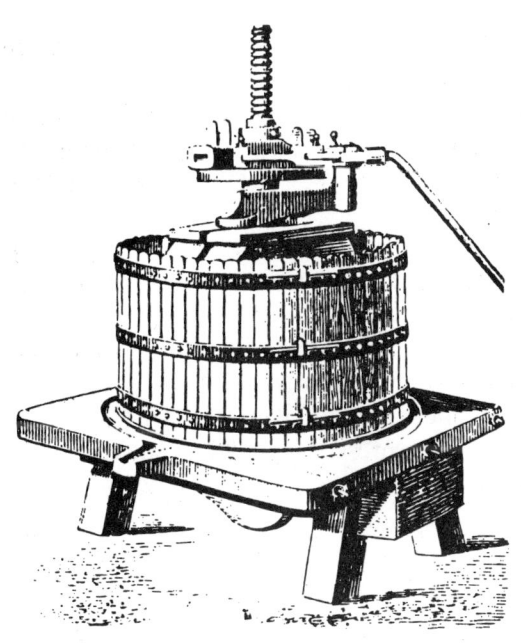

THE CULTURAL AND VINICULTURAL MILIEU OF MR. SHERLOCK HOLMES

It is the custom and joy of Holmesians to re-create the Victorian era in all its exuberance or repression, depending upon our natural predispositions. We scavenge for authentic costumes, decorate our apartments and chateaux with dark plush, and treasure small tokens from a past we share only with Mr. Holmes. To hold a smooth, faceless, nineteenth century shilling delights us, and our Earl Grey tastes better from cups emblazoned with a likeness of Victoria, our Queen. These tangible mementoes help us create a world from the outside in. The flash of a simulated blue carbuncle, the tinkling of china cups, and the rustle and sheen of a satin petticoat provide us, if only for a moment, with a texture of times past.

We can also transform our imaginings into reality by creating the Holmesian world from the inside out; to paraphrase the dictum of Brillat-Savarin: "You are what you drink."

A tendency to use contemporary standards of taste as a basis for discourse flaws much of the previous scholarship dealing with Mr. Holmes's vinous tastes and fancies. The names Latour, Lafite, and La Romanée-Conti liberally sprinkle these writings, which attribute to the Great Detective preferences and attitudes of a present day wine snob. Sadly, they demonstrate a lack of understanding of the cultural and vinicultural milieu in which Mr. Holmes lived.

Textual evidence (Holmes's family history and Watson's comments upon his friend's philosophical viewpoint) examined in conjunction with the economic and agricultural reality of the Victorian period provide a clear picture of Mr. Holmes's personal approach to wine: definitely no wine snob, he!

Let us consider the detective's lineage. French in the blood takes the strangest forms. The French are, and always have been, quaffers rather than keepers, choosing as a rule modest wines for daily drinking: a nice little Bordeaux with steak and frites, a decent Chablis with sole, a refreshing rose with conversation. Baron Phillipe de Rothschild shared this traditional Gallic wisdom. When asked to name the proper food to eat with his famous wine, he replied:

> "Developing your taste is one of the pleasures of the game and if you finish up drinking Mouton with Irish Stew and Champagne with spaghetti, it seems to me entirely your own affair."

A thorough examination of the Holmesian canon reveals the detective's sympathy with the good Baron's attitude. Whilst he undoubtedly appreciates a fine bottle of claret or an attractive Burgundy he never treats the matter with the pathological obsession of the snob. Only three wines are mentioned by name: Montrachet, Beaune, and Tokay and there is but a passing reference to a famous vintage. For the most part, he chooses simple and sound wines, by far the wisest approach considering the chaotic state of the European wine market of the period.

During the late nineteenth and early twentieth centuries wine producers and negociants throughout Europe faced continual crisis. Vine disease followed by ruinous infestation wreaked irrevocable havoc.

This massive devastation resulted from *phylloxera vastatrix*, an insect whose fiendish lifestyle makes it neigh-well impossible to arrest. This brazen bug, it is conjectured, found its way from America to a greenhouse in Hammersmith on the leaves of an ornamental shrub. By 1868 it had infected the vineyards of Bordeaux; by 1884 it had destroyed most of viticultural France and had crippled Austro-Hungary, Germany, Spain, Italy, Portugal and Madeira.

The phylloxera scourge continued unabated until the late 1880s when scientists developed a method of combatting the pernicious pest. The process involved grafting vine scions on to Phylloxera-resistant American rootstock. Phylloxera-free vintages did not appear until the early 1890s.

Checking the vintage notations from 1849 to 1910 in Michael Broadbent's *Great Vintage Wine Book*, we discover that only fifteen of the sixty-one vintages received a designation of 'high quality', 'good', or 'outstanding'. Broadbent describes eleven of the sixty-one as 'bad', 'not very attractive', 'charmless' and even 'worst of the century' .

The thirsty English public cared not a whit for the tribulations of the Continental vintner. They expected business as usual and they got the business, as usual.

The French handled the problem of English demand and shortage of supply as they had traditionally dealt with the English wine market: extensive blending and no little sleight-of-hand.

Long before phylloxera contaminated the soil, the practical French had adulterated the wines of their most famous regions to suit the taste of the English consumer. In 1836 Cyrus Redding, one of the first in a long line of fine English wine writers, described the practice:

> The first growths of Medoc are never sent to England in a perfect state, but are, when destined for that market, mingled with other wines and with spirits of wine. The taste of a pure wine is not spirituous enough for the English palate, and more body is given these by the mixture of Hermitage, or Beni Carlos from Spain, and alcohol, ordinarily to the extent of three or four-twentieths per cent. By this means all the delicate flavour, the delicious and salutary quality of the wine is destroyed to give it a warmer and more intoxicating effect, without which in England these wines would not find a market... Natural and healthful wines, the genuine offspring of simple fermentation, are not the fashion in England; hence artificial means must be used to please an artificial taste.

The French moved easily from adulterating wine to adulterating grape juice. In *Burgundy*, Anthony Hanson tells us that, during the phylloxera crisis, French negociants shipped grape juice from other countries, which they then blended with blood, chemicals and sugar, to sell in England as Burgundy and claret.

Even a knowledgeable and discerning buyer could not be sure that what he tasted and selected in the fine morning sun of a foreign seaport would be the same product the seller poured into barrels for delivery.

The mercantile custom of bait-and-switch has a long and infamous history.

The difficult conditions under which wines made their way from the producing countries to England must also be taken into account. Stowed in the hold of ships in wooden casks, called hogsheads, the wine was subjected to the vagaries of climate and crew. Cheaper than water and a prophylactic against scurvy, a ration of wine was issued to each crewman to help him through the long voyage. Mariners have an almost proverbial propensity for drink, and often stole a swig or three of the wine intended for sale, covering the theft by topping up the barrel with whatever came to hand.

Often oxidation set in before the wine was even bottled. The Château Bottling Pact of 1905, signed by representatives from Châteaux Haut-Brion, Latour, Margaux and the Rothschilds, marked the first serious attempt to put an end to the twin evils of spoilage and tampering. Not all vineyards, however, had fine reputations to protect and undoubtedly, by the time most wine reached the docks at Liverpool it was more pestiferous than pure.

The chicanery did not cease once the wine reached England, the standing rule of the time being, the stronger the better. To the uninitiated eye, stronger meant darker. The conscientious wine merchant intent on giving the public what it wanted devised all sorts of clever ways to darken and strengthen his red wine.

He, too, added blood, which not only darkens but thickens! Dried lemon peel can add that piquant quality sought after in certain wines. For mature clarets, a few hours in the oven does the trick. Violet powder and rough cider certainly add complexity to a thin Bordeaux.

Once the average Englishman had toted his bottle of Château Le Plonk home he subjected it to all kinds of barbarism in the name of fashion and connoisseurship. The concept of 'room temperature', for example, ignored the differences in climate between, say, south-western France and Manchester. To achieve hypothetical French room temperature, the English heated their wine. A clever manufacturer, his finger on the bibulous public's pulse, brought out a line of 'marsupial' bottles. Conveniently attached pouches held hot coals which brought the wine to 'correct' temperature. These handy items were all the rage in the mid-1800s. Gentlemen unable or unwilling to invest in marsupials sat their bottles next to the roaring grate, roasting the wine beyond recognition.

All this is not to say that decent wines were not to be had from British vintners. A small band of merchants who dealt with the *élite*, began to request wines that were purer, or at least, less 'enhanced'. The Englishman with a palate and a passion for wine depended upon his merchant's generosity and wisdom.

It must be noted that every proud cellar owner had barrels and bottles of Port, Sherry and Madeira, wines which offer, perhaps, the most representative taste of the Victorian period. They are heady, full, sensual, and considered just a trifle old-fashioned by those who have no memory of a past. Each carries with it its own rituals and traditions, offering us gracious pleasures, precious glimpses of our shared history. Aromas that fill the senses and linger, serene, seductive; rich hues infused with brilliant highlights; tastes that speak of warm southern climates on cold winter nights; such are the pleasures of fortified wines.

Their capacity for aging allows us to pull the cork on a fine Vintage Port, a sultry amontillado or a nineteenth century Madeira and breathe the air of Mr. Holmes's time: dense as London fog, fragrant as the Queen's garden, and rich as our imaginations.

A CASE OF IDENTITY

The Essence of Tokay

> "It's a good wine."
> "A remarkable wine, Watson."
> Dr J. H. Watson and Mr Sherlock Holmes
> *His Last Bow*

Only one wine has been known to move Mr. Sherlock Holmes to such fulsome praise. I should like to elucidate what I believe to be this nectar's provenance. The wine Mr. Holmes drank from that heavily sealed, dust-covered bottle in *His Last Bow* and, further, the wine Mr. Thaddeus Sholto offered to Miss Mary Morstan in *The Sign of Four* can be none other than Hungarian Imperial Tokay.

Familiarity breeds content. When confronted with the prickly thicket of ampelographical nomenclature many scholars have taken the easily travelled path. The Tokay most available to contemporary imbibers and scholars is Tokay d'Alsace, a wine made from Pinot Gris grapes. Since this wine is usually dry and by contemporary standards a liking for dry styles connotes sophistication, they conclude that this is the wine the Great Detective enjoyed.

This fails to consider the availability of Alsace wines in England during Mr. Holmes's lifetime. "I have often wondered where Alsace wines went before they hit Paris in the 1960s," muses Giles MacDonogh, polymath and occasional contributor the *Financial Times*. "Honest men there (there are not many) allude to contacts with the Courts of Baden and Wurttemberg, where they would have spoken the same Allemanic German. Some of it travelled down the Rhine, where, I suspect it was relabelled as German wine. Modern transport has made the reputation of Alsace wines. The Vosges were virtually unpassable, as the French discovered to their chagrin in the Great War."

The Germans, who controlled the territories of Alsace and Lorraine from 1871 until 1918, were interested in achieving maximum yield from the vineyards, not maintaining quality production. The onset of phylloxera speeded their advancement toward this goal. They ordered that ravaged vines be replaced with hybrid direct producers. Such vines are resistant to infestation and are able to produce a large quantity of low quality grapes. Wines from overcropped vines of this type are invariably insipid. When the region reverted to French dominion at the end of the war, its citizens were faced with the long and arduous task of replanting, a process not completed until the end of World War II.

In *His Last Bow* Mr. Holmes links the name Tokay to that of Franz Josef. The Austrian Court lost its fondness for Alsace wines in 1683 when the region was annexed by Louis XIV. With the Austrian's subsequent appropriation of estates in the Tokay hills there was little need to go as far afield as northeastern France for Pinot Gris as the vine had been cultivated in Hungary, under the name of Szurkebarat, since 1375.

In 1568 Baron Lazare de Schwendi, a colonel in the Imperial Army added considerably to the already tangled appellatial skein when he brought cuttings of Pinot Gris, which he christened Tokay, from Hungary to his estates in Alsace.

Hungarian Tokay is a blend of Harslevelu, Furmint, and Yellow Muscat and takes its name from Tokaji, a town nestled in the curve of the Bodrog river. Autumnal mists swirl through the hillside vineyards, encouraging the development of *botrytis cinerea*, the fungus that creates Sauternes, Trockenbeerenauslese and other renowned dessert wines.

The records of a lawsuit filed by workers objecting to the extra labour involved in separating the Trockenbeeren from the healthy grapes proves that Tokay, as we know it, originated in the mid-seventeenth century.

There is no question that it is Hungarian Tokay Mr. Holmes admired, as the wine is clearly identified in the text of *His Last Bow*. "Another glass, Watson," said Mr. Sherlock Holmes as he extended the bottle of Imperial Tokay.

The clincher is the word Imperial. In *The Story of Wine*, Hugh Johnson proclaims, "The Tokay known as Imperial and drunk by the Emperors in Vienna was the Aszu blended with a measure of the Essence."

Essencia (a.k.a. Essence and Essenzia) is the rich, sweet, free-run juice of grapes infected by *botrytis cinerea* (noble rot). Aszu is the wine produced from treading the pulpy remains of the nobly rotten grapes mixed with the must of unaffected grapes.

Mr. Holmes goes on to declare: "Our friend upon the sofa has assured me that it is from Franz Josef's special cellar at the Schoenbrunn Palace."

"It is entirely plausible that Franz Josef would have held stocks at Schoenbrunn," author-historian Stephen Brooks assures me. "Indeed, I have a bottle (empty) of 1901 Imperial Tokay that might well have had such a source."

The Austrian Court had long taken a special interest in Hungarian Tokay. In 1779 the Empress Maria Theresa issued a law governing its production. In 1784, her son, Josef II, imposed a tax on wines from Tokay and Rust (which was often passed off as Tokay). In 1823 further legislation prescribed punishments for winemakers who concocted Tokay from honey and raisins. Franz Josef would have been no different from his ancestors.

He is known to have routinely given dozens of bottles of Tokay to Queen Victoria on her birthday. This expensive gesture undoubtedly found favour with the Empress of India as she was certainly cognizant of Tokay's remarkable properties.

"Nor will I mince matters and refrain from saying that when childless families despair, January is wed to May, and when old men wish to be young again, then Tokay is in request," writes Dr. Robert Druitt, MRCP, in the pamphlet he dedicated to Gladstone.

Dr. Druitt tells us that a mixture of Tokay and cream, "sometimes soothe[s] a dying bed and enable[s] an old man to forget the peevishness of suffering and to bless his family tranquilly before he falls into his last sleep."

If administered promptly Tokay can, it would seem, awaken one from that eternal slumber. In 1933, C. W. Berry, a director of Berry Brothers & Rudd, vintners to persons of the better sort, proclaimed the following: "A medical man, and a friend, who had sneered at the suggestion to try this wine in a case of extreme illness, actually put a little in a man's mouth... when he really had come to the conclusion he had passed away. My friend told me afterward that the effect was like an electric shock - the old gentleman is alive today, and, believe me, this is no fairy tale."

Mr. Berry goes on to explain the exceptional longevity of Pope Leo XlII: "I will tell you what kept him alive - Tokay Essence sent to him direct from the Emperor of Austria. I believe that I am correct in saying that for the last six or eight weeks of his life, nothing passed his lips save this immortal liquor."

I believe we can agree that Hungarian Tokay is a truly remarkable wine.

My final evidence is of a subjective but none the less valid nature. It involves the character of the men in the canon who own and appreciate the wine: Von Bork, Sholto and Mr. Holmes himself.

For the German, Von Bork, an appreciation of Tokay was bred in the bone. Peter the Great of Russia and Frederick I of Prussia figured among the wine's many passionate devotees. Vienna, Moscow, Berlin, St. Petersburg, Warsaw and Prague were its major markets.

Von Bork considers himself a superior creature. He displays this in the ennui with which he shrugs off Von Herling's predictions of the hero's welcome awaiting him in Berlin, as well as in the indifference with which he confides the combination of his safe to Mr. Holmes. Such a man would only deem worthy of his esteem a wine that bears the motto: *Vinum Regum, Rex Vinorum*.

I believe Thaddeus Sholto shares this sense of superiority. The word connoisseur rolls easily off the tongues of both men. Like true connoisseurs they are ready to offer their treasures to valued guests.

Sitting in his 'oasis of art in the howling desert of South London' surrounded by the richest and glossiest curtains and tapestries, richly mounted paintings, oriental vases, and thick moss-soft carpet, Thaddeus Sholto imagines himself the Pukka Sahib of his tiny domain.

With his predilection for oriental luxury, Tokay d'Alsace, even in the luscious style known as *Selection de Grains Nobles*, lacks the opulence and exoticism that Mr. Sholto's psyche craves. A legendary elixir sipped by monarchs and Popes would be more in keeping with his *Selbstanschauung*.

We must also consider the delicate state of Mr. Sholto's health. Surely this self-avowed valetudinarian would be well aware of the revivifying powers attributed to Hungarian Tokay and take every opportunity to avail himself of a restoring tot.

To Mr. Holmes I ascribe no base motives for his admiration. His appreciation springs from the simple yet profound pleasure that comes from tasting a first-class wine. It is the taste of a wine and not its aura that a true connoisseur seeks to experience.

For Dr. Druitt, Tokay has "a flavour of green tea, but an amalgam of the scents of meadowsweet, acacia blossom and the lime tree flower."

"In Tokay there is a bouquet that is as subtle to the tongue as Oloroso Sherry and when you have quaffed it the fragrance seems to possess overtones that resound like a note echoing on the piano strings through all their harmonies," rhapsodies Walter Starkie, author of such classics as *Raggle-Taggle* and *Don Gypsy*.

It offers Hugh Johnson "silky texture, a haunting fragrance and the flavour of mingled fruit and butter and caramel and the breath of the Bodrog among October vines."

Although served 'at table' by Emperors, the task of matching Tokay with food proves to be a sticky problem for contemporary aficionados. The ebullient Walter Starkie believes it is "a sacrilege to drink the golden liquid while seated at a table."

He feels "it should be drunk when wandering beneath trees listening to [the] music... it is the wine to drink when the *Tzigan* tunes his fiddle and the dark girl by your side waits for the rhythmic impulse of the *czardas*." Quite!

Others suggest it be treated in the same way as Sauternes and served with desserts. Of course, the most famous pairing of Sauternes is with *foie gras*. Is it too fanciful to suggest that a distinctive slender-necked, half-litre bottle of Tokay featured among the group of ancient and cobwebby bottles Mr. Holmes ordered to accompany his epicurean cold supper? For what would better complement a slice of *pâté de foie gras* pie than a brimming glass of Imperial Tokay?

SHALL I OPEN A FLASK?

The Cellar of Mr. Thaddeus Sholto

"May I offer you a glass of Chianti, Miss Morstan?
Or of Tokay? I keep no other wines."
Mr Thaddeus Sholto
The Sign of Four

Precious, opulent Hungarian Tokay's place in the heart and cellar of Mr. Thaddeus Sholto is easily understood, but the gentleman's choice of Chianti may seem obscure. However, his criteria for selecting these two wines is the same: both have long and illustrious histories, have enjoyed prestigious patronage and both have bona fide medicinal value.

The towns of Florence and Sienna, in the heart of the Chianti zone, have for centuries been centres, not only of wine production, but also of culture, art and politics. When Michelangelo was at Rome, he often wrote to his nephew to send him flasks of the wine from Florence. In the mid-fifteenth century Chianti wine inspired Leonardo da Vinci to design the distinctive straw basket that covers its flasks. Goethe sipped the wine on his *Italienische Reise* and Robert Browning made Elizabeth merry with tumblers full of the wine which she described as 'an excellent kind of claret'.

As early as the ninth century the great Medical School at Salerno advised its patients: "Wine, if pure, gives you many benefits: it comforts the brain, soothes the stomach, removes noxious vapours from your body, relaxes a full belly, sharpens your wits, nurtures your sight and clarifies your hearing, strengthens your body and makes your limbs robust". Of particular interest to the valetudinarian Mr. Sholto, the school recommends patients suffering from chest pains (*angina pectoris*) take a glass of red wine at intervals throughout the day.

But not all red wines are created equal. Bordeaux wines, the natural choice for an Englishman's cellar, when destined for Britain were often adulterated with flavouring agents and with stronger, darker wines and spirits. Whilst this satisfied the demands of the market it would hardly suit Mr. Sholto's need for purity and desire for salubrity.

Phylloxera did not devastate Italian vineyards as it did France. Massive planting of new sites was undertaken as the Italians sought to profit from France's woes. From 1870 to 1890 Italy's wine production doubled. In 1880 80% of the population made its living from vinegrowing, winemaking and trading. These newly planted areas satisfied the demand for plonk whilst the established wine regions of Italy, with illustrious histories to preserve, maintained their traditional high standards. In Chianti, the most prestigious of the many excellent houses were (and are) Brolio, Antinori and Frescobaldi. It is from amongst these three producers that we shall find Mr. Sholto's Chianti .

Baron Bettino Riscasoli, a true *noblesse d'epée*, inherited the Brolio estate in the heart of Chianti Classico in the mid-nineteenth century. He zealously set about perfecting his wine and promoting international commerce. However, Brolio wines did not line Mr. Sholto's cellar, for the Baron's political aspirations supplanted his interest in œnology .

When he became prime minister of Tuscany in 1860, royalty and diplomats flocked to the region, many of whom developed a taste for Chianti. Mr. Henry A. Lagard, a minister in the service of Queen Victoria was amongst them. He wrote to the Antinori family from Venice in 1876: "Tell the Marchese Antinori that my friends and I prefer your wines to all the wines we've found here, including those of Bordeaux."

The Antinori family has traded in wine since the fourteenth century and has owned vineyards in the Classico zone from the sixteenth century. The firm - in the modern sense - was created in 1895. Although not commercially available, Mr. Sholto could have imported the wine through a member of the diplomatic corps. But it was not an Antinori wine that he offered to Miss Morstan.

The house of Frescobaldi is as ancient and respected as that of Antinori. The family dynasty was founded in the fouteenth century; its fortunes derived from the lucrative trade in fabrics and from money lending. The Frescobaldis owned the Florentine bank that financed King Edward II and Isabella of France's lavish wedding celebration in 1307 at which, it must be added, 1,152,000 bottles of wine (Bordeaux) were consumed.

Frescobaldi di Nipozzano was the wine Mr. Sholto sipped and savoured. This wine is different from the others we have discussed. It does not come from the Classico zone but rather from Rufina, the smallest sub-district of Chianti. Maureen Ashley, M.W. writes: "Rufina has sound claims to be held in high consideration; as high or higher, dare I say, than the Classico."

Further, the wine of Nipozzano were singled out in the 1800s by Doctor Paola Mantegazza who advised convalescents to drink this *tonico genuino*.

Chianti and Tokay, therefore, form a perfect pair. In common they share an appeal to the sensual nature of poets and artists, a noble heritage, and each is imbued with exceptional medicinal qualities. Yet their flavour, weight and style offer quite different and distinct pleasures. Mr. Thaddeus Sholto chose his wines with supreme logic. They satisfy him completely - body and soul. Indeed, he need keep no other wines.

ANCIENT AND COBWEBBY BOTTLES

...a quite epicurean little cold supper began to be laid out upon our humble lodging-house mahogany. There were a couple of brace of cold woodcock, a pheasant, *pâté de foie gras* pie with a group of ancient and cobwebby bottles.
The Adventure of the Noble Bachelor

The striking silhouette of that collection of bottles stands bold in the imagination of eager œnophiles. 'Ancient and cobwebby': the very phrase stirs within us the desire to each vessel toward the fading autumnal light and examine it more closely. By employing the deductive methods so well known to the daughters and sons (figuratively speaking) of Mr. Sherlock Holmes, I shall endeavour to illuminate the provenance of this illustrious quintet.

The chronicle of Mr. Holmes's existence never dwells on great vintages and prestigious names for the simple reason that Mr. Holmes never made much of them. Watson would not have spared us a mention of a passion for purchasing and contemplating wines had it existed, for such a passion is truly a consuming one.

That is not to say that Mr. Holmes eschewed the pleasures of exceptional wines when they came his way. Nor does it imply that he would have been unable to make informed decisions when organizing epicurean suppers of the sort that sent Dr. Watson's imagination racing into the exotic territory of the Arabian Nights.

The good doctor's awestruck references to genii and luxury and a mysteriously pre-paid bill lead us to the logical conclusion that no expense was spared on this occasion; this provides us with the first clue to the identification of the wines.

Further the wines must compliment the menu and consider the tastes of the guests and the times; they must be 'ancient' in relation to 1888 and cobwebby, which carries with it the implication of long cellaring; and they should be on the market and thus available to the extraordinary confectioner who supplies them.

The noted œnologist, Professor Émile Peynaud, amongst other winelovers and gastronomes, recommends that very old or light red wines be drunk with small game birds. Traditionally unhung birds, such as grouse, quail and partridge, are served with red Bordeaux.

For hung game, such as the pheasant on our menu, the time-honoured partner is red Burgundy.

Burgundies are generally approachable at an earlier age than claret. It should also be remembered that in Mr. Holmes's times these wines were higher in alcohol. For example, a contemporary Corton's alcohol level is 12.5%; an 1858 Corton had an alcohol level of 15.6%. These wines reached maturity at between 25 and 30 years after the vintage. Professor Saintsbury enjoyed an 1858 Romanée Conti when it was 25 years old and found it 'absolute perfection'.

Two Burgundies, both from the Côte de Beaune, are mentioned in the Canon: Montrachet, a white wine and Beaune, a name which can apply to either reds or whites from the zone.

The classification of the Côte d'Or prepared in 1861 by Dr. Jules Lavalle for the Comité d'Agriculture de Beaune for the Paris Exposition Universelle listed only one red Grand Cru in the Côte de Beaune: Corton.

Three vintages had reached the appropriate level of development to enhance a supper held in 1888 and they may all be considered *grande année*. They are the 1858, 1864 and the 1865.

An 1865 Corton tasted in September, 1988, surprised me with its elegant fruit and firm structure. The nose was clean and fragrant. It was the waning shadow of the fresh, rich, juicy mouthful that Mr. Holmes and his guests enjoyed in its prime.

There are those who would plump for white Burgundy in this spot. "For the purist, for the dedicated connoisseur," says Michael Broadbent, "white Burgundy is the wine that precedes and compliments claret at table." In its favour is Mr. Holmes's taste for something choice in white wines.

Although best with chicken and fish, Mr. Holmes is known to have served white Burgundy with partridge and quite likely he served it with grouse; some may reason that he would have reckoned this wine an acceptable partner for pheasant. But this overlooks the dramatic differences in the flavour and aromas of hung and unhung game. The pheasant is intensely pungent, quite unlike the partridge.

Also against the choice of a white Burgundy is the matter of vintage. Most white Burgundies should be drunk when they are young and fresh; the notable exceptions are Corton-Charlemagne and Montrachet. The oldest vintage presented under Mr. Holmes's instruction that evening would have been the 1878, a year of refined and well-constructed wines. The English have always taken perverse pleasure in sipping wines that have slipped over the line from maturity to decrepitude and such wines are fine if one wants to sit and ponder, but they would never do as an accompaniment for a game bird. We must remember Mr. Holmes's French ancestry; he surely would not have chosen a white Burgundy - even a Montrachet - of over ten years to complement a meal, and ten is much too tender an age to be classified as 'Ancient and Cobwebby'.

A couple of brace of cold woodcock have been laid upon the mahogany. They need a well-structured wine to match their rich, dark, gamey flavours: claret is the traditional partner.

In 1888 Bordeaux wines from Pomerol and St-Émilion were virtually unknown in Britain. The Bordeaux hierarchy, established by 1811 and codified in the 1855 Classification, ranked the wines of Lafite, Latour, Margaux and Haut Brion as the best, and that is what the British demanded.

The confectioner, acting under the instructions of Mr. Holmes, would have chosen from amongst these august wines one that pays tribute to the antecedent of the former Miss Hatty Doran, by setting on the table a bottle of Haut Brion, known by anglophones for centuries by the endearing moniker: O'Brian.

In 1660, the estate's owner, Arnaud de Pontac, went against local wisdom by actively wooing the British market rather than simply slaking Dutch thirst. In 1666 de Pontac sent his son to London to create a fashionable restaurant that would feature his wines. The plan succeeded admirably. The New Eating House, as it was pithily called, attracted a refined clientele which included besides rich merchants, businessmen and aristocrats, the likes of Daniel Defoe, Jonathan Swift, and John Locke.

Under de Pontac's direction Haut Brion became the first Bordeaux to be sold under the name of the estate.

On 10th April, 1663, Mr. Samuel Pepys noted in his famous diary: "[I] drank a sort of French wine called 'Ho Bryan', that hath a good and most particular taste that I ever met with."

In 1788 Mr. Thomas Jefferson, the great wine connoisseur and gourmet, wrote in a letter to Mr. Francis Eppes: "I cannot deny myself the pleasure of asking you to participate of a parcel of wine I have been choosing for myself. I do it... as it will furnish you a specimen of what is the very best Bordeaux wine. It is... Obrian."

Unlike today's early maturing Bordeaux, the wines of Mr. Holmes's time needed long ageing to reach drinkability.

In the 1960s, Hugh Johnson, promulgator of fine wine-drinking, tasted an 1899 Haut Brion. "Its scent rose firmly to a peak like the pediment of the Parthenon. Below it were great depths of taste. It was pure delight of a kind which only the greatest wines, or music, or poetry, or painting can give."

As for the vintage Mr. Holmes drank, we must hark back to the first great claret vintage, the magnificent Comet year of 1811.

Michael Broadbent describes a first growth from this vintage as "drinking gracefully at the age of 115."

My reasons for selecting this prodigious vintage are twofold. First, at an ennobled 77 it satisfies Dr. Watson's age requirement whilst still offering a wine in vigorous middle age, quite capable of enhancing the dark meat of woodcock. The second reason hinges upon the doctor's literary skills. Let me remind you that the supper we are discussing occurred a few weeks before his marriage.

Set a few months after his marriage, *The Stock Broker's Clerk* contains the following passage:

> Then Sherlock Holmes cocked his eye at me, leaning back on the cushions with a pleased and yet critical face, like a connoisseur who has just taken his first sip of a comet vintage.

Doctor Watson's narrative abilities have been discussed at length elsewhere. Suffice it to say, that I do not believe that he could have described this precise moment of epiphany without actually having observed it.

The third bottle set on the table that evening was the immortal Hungarian Tokay. A 1790 tasted in September, 1987, is described by Michael Broadbent as: "Deep, rich warm amber, mahogany shading to olive rim; magnificent old bouquet, sweet, supple, raisiny; sweet, full bodied, excellent honey and raisiny flavour, good length, excellent acidity keeping it vigorous."

As in Sauternes, a portion of the grapes used to make Imperial Tokay becomes infected with *botrytis cinerea*. These nobly rotten grapes, with their highly concentrated flavours impart a distinctive taste to the wine. The traditional pairing of Sauternes and *foie gras* leads me to conclude that Imperial Tokay would suit the fanciful *pâté de foie gras* pie. There is another element that suggest that Tokay featured on the menu that evening: another mould, as it happens.

The magnificent cellars carved into the sides of the Tokaji mountains create an environment that encourages the development of the most exquisite fungus. Its soft, grey, wispy and clings tenaciously to every bottle of Tokay. Surely it was this mould that inspired Dr. Watson to remark upon the 'cobwebby' bottles.

Two other wines graced the table that evening: Champagne, the most fashionable wine of the mid-Victorian era, and, after the cloth was removed, Madeira.

A study of Christie's auction catalogues from the Victorian to the Edwardian period reveals the most fashionable grande marque Champagnes to be Ayala, Delbeck, Irroy, Veuve-Clicquot, Moët, Pommery and, above all, Perrier-Jouet. The now celebrated names of Krug and Bollinger did not appear.

Traditionally the English have appreciated mature champagne, finding pleasure in the challenge of an older wine. However, wine aficionados - past and present - recognize that after fifteen years champagne begins to lose its festive, sparkling nature.

Vintages younger than 1879 would as yet not have been released or deemed too young to drink. The years from 1875 to 1879 ranged from poor to disastrous and can therefore be eliminated from consideration. This leaves the most renowned vintage of the period, 1874.

The '74 Perrier-Jouet sold for up to 780 shillings per dozen in 1887 at Christie's auction house. According to Michael Broadbent, this was "an unprecedented price, many times that of a first growth claret and a level not exceeded for any wine until 1967."

Professor George Saintsbury, a noted imbiber and contemporary of Mr. Holmes, had some 1874 Perrier-Jouet "just in perfection, ten years old, all rawness gone, but sparkle in fullest force." The professor mixed this wine with an older vintage to achieve the softer elegance he sought. That would not have been necessary in 1888 when the wine would have been mature, yet still vivacious and crisp.

Could the spirited Mrs Francis Hay Moulton and her soul-mate be toasted with anything less?

"Many people declare, and quite rightly too," says Mr. C. W. Berry, "that they cannot take Port on top of Champagne. Let them try Madeira - Madeira old and good - and they will not regret it."

Without doubt, the after dinner wine that evening was Madeira, a wine well-known and greatly appreciated in the United States. It would appeal to the robust tastes of the American guests and reinforce Mr. Holmes's empathy with things American.

Madeira, one of the world's longest lived wines, could certainly provide an 'ancient' vintage to satisfy Dr. Watson.

Professor Saintsbury, pooh-poohed any vintage after 1850, the year oidium struck the island. The professor drank a "1780 Madeira when it was nearly ninety years old and in perfection - it was a thing to say grace for and remember."

My tasting note, made in October of 1985, for an 1789 Bual describes the wine as: Rich, green-tea tinged dark-amber. Heady, intense perfumes, hints of roast almonds. Toasty. Excellent, crisp acidity balanced by medium sweetness. Velvety textures. Exquisite long, lingering finish.

Ah, that's how a meal should end. In our bright imaginings, let us draw the cork, fill our glasses and inhale the rich, heady scents of an autumn evening in Baker Street.

A COMET YEAR

Comets have always inspired a mystical awe in human kind, leaving in their wake eddying vapours of fortune and fate. Political alliances, earthquakes, and exceptional harvests all have been attributed to the passing of these celestial streakers.

Comets do produce strange weather conditions, including eruptions of volcanos and it is certainly true that large comets passing near the earth exercise measurable gravitational pull.

The celebration of auspicious comet years reached its peak with the passing of the largest ever recorded: The Great Comet of 1811. Its diameter was calculated at around 1.25 million miles whilst its tail extended for over a hundred million miles. This magnificent specimen loomed bright in the sky for several months.

It was discovered by Honoré Flaugergues on 26th March, 1811, and its last reported sighting was in Russia on 17th August, 1812.

The harvests throughout Europe during this comet's visit were outstanding and the Champagne houses were inspired to adopt the custom of branding their corks with the comet symbol, no doubt hoping this would bring equally good vintages in years to come.

When a connoisseur speaks of the 1811 it is always under the honourable title of The Comet Vintage.

Drawing by Weedon Grossmith for *The Diary of a Nobody*

VINTAGE CHARTS

Holmes smiled and rubbed his hands. We were, may I say, seated in the old sitting room of the ancient hotel, with a bottle of the famous vintage of which Holmes had spoken on the table between us.
The Adventure of the Creeping Man

What follows are the good to great vintages Mr. Holmes may have had occasion to taste.

CLARET

We had a pleasant little meal together, during which Holmes would talk about nothing but violins, narrating with great exaltation how he had purchased his own Stradivarius, which was worth at least five hundred guineas, at a Jew Broker's in Tottenham Court Road for fifty-five shillings. This led him to Paganini, and we sat for an hour over a bottle of claret while he told me anecdote after

> anecdote of that extraordinary man. The afternoon was far advanced and the hot glare had softened into a mellow glow before we found ourselves at the police-station.
> *The Adventure of the Cardboard Box*

1811 The famous Comet Vintage. Considered by some to be the finest claret ever made. Michael Broadbent found that Lafite 1811 was "drinking gracefully at the age of 115."

1815 Good.

1825 Very Fine vintage. It followed a string of very bad years. Michael Broadbent tasted a Château Gruaud-Larose from this vintage in 1977. Here is his note: "Surprisingly deep plummy colour, not bright as it had no time to settle; very rich old Cabernet aroma, ripe mulberry, just a touch of decay; a ripeness on the palate, lovely rich flavour leading to a light dry finish."

1841 Excellent year. "Much liked in England... Prices moderate until the quality became known, and then very high." (From the summary record kept by the *regisseurs* at Château Lafite.)

1844 Fine. Often compared with the 1815s.

1848 Good.

1858 Exceptional Quality. It followed a string of very bad years.

1864 Superb vintage. Michael Broadbent described the wines as "of pronounced bouquet, sap, finesse, softness and elegance." Warner Allen said of an 1864 Lafite: "it was like passing from fine prose to the inspiration of poetry."

1865 Splendid year. "Wines full of colour body and all the characteristics of *une grande année*." said Michael Broadbent.

1869 Very fine quality. Of an 1869 C. W. Berry declaimed: "Now the band begins to play - there's music in every drop."

1870 One of the greatest pre-phylloxera vintages. The wines when young were exceptionally massive and unyielding. It took 50 years or more for them to become drinkable.

1874 High quality. "The important thing with 1874 Lafite," says Michael Broadbent, "is to taste the wine in its historical context... in 1874 the Impressionists were painting, Brahms was composing and Paris was just over the Commune."

1878 Very good wines, according to Michael Broadbent. André Simon assessed them as follows: "Doubtful at first, quality greatly improved with time".

1893 Good quality. It followed 15 discouraging vintages.

1896 Good. Light wines.

1899 Outstanding. *Trés Grande Année*. C.W. Berry found the St Émilion and Graves "indeed delectable".

1900 Outstanding.

1920 The first unqualified *Grande Année* after 1900.

1910 to 1919 was a thoroughly miserable period in Bordeaux. André Simon tells of a lone exception:
" ...even in 1910, which was by far the worst vintage of the ten. Haut Brion provided probably the one exception to the rule out of all '10s. Maurice Healy, always the champion of lost causes and 'outside' vintages, loved to served Haut Brion '10 at the Windham Club and to make wine experts among his friends and mentors apologize to the 1910 vintage for damning it as a thoroughly 'rotten' year; and they apologized and drank Healy's Haut Brion '10 with incredulity and without shame."

RED BURGUNDY

"By Jove!" I cried, "if he really wants someone to share the rooms and the expense,
I am the very man for him.
I should prefer having a partner to being alone."
Young Stamford looked rather strangely at me over his wineglass. "You don't know Sherlock Holmes yet," he said; "perhaps you would not care for him as a constant companion."
A Study in Scarlet

1858 Good. A Corton, Clôs du Roi tasted in 1967 by Michael Broadbent was: "lively, meaty, fruity bouquet; faded, light but sound, clean and attractive. Very good for its age."

1859 Outstanding.

1864 Outstanding. Mr. Broadbent tasted an 1864 Beaune in 1974: "Very attractive colour, fading, of course, and autumnal, but with a healthy blush of red; gentle old Pinot bouquet; soft, delicate, no decay, slightly roasted end taste."

1865 One of the greatest mid-century vintages. André Simon: "The last time I enjoyed a '65 Burgundy was in January, 1938... [it] was superb - old, of course, but sound to the core and gracious to the end."

1869 Very fine.

1870 Very fine.

1875 Great vintage. A Romanée Conte from this vintage tasted by André Simon in 1937, "stands fresh in [his] memory as Burgundy *in excelsis*; absolutely perfect, delicate, almost ethereal and, of course, free from all trace of acetic acid, mustiness or any other form of decay: yet it came after a Cheval Blanc 1921, a Goliath of a wine which this lithe David faced unafraid and laid low."

1878 Outstanding. Refined well-structured.

1886 Good. A La Tâche '86 tasted by André Simon in 1931: "Its colour was still beautiful; it had plenty of body left, and a surprising, as well as rather attractive, bitter-sweet finish, with a curious nutty flavour."

1887 Good. C. W. Berry: "This... Clôs de Vougeot... is indeed a dream."

1904 Very good. "The '04s," says André Simon, "were so good that it seems hardly fair not to place their vintage in the front rank of the best years of the century."

1909 Fair. "Some of the '09s were pleasant wines when they were young, but they acquired a faint bitterness with age and a more objectionable rabbit hutch bouquet at a later stage, both of which were true enough witnesses to the wines' honourable old age," says André Simon, "but not the sort of witness that I wish to see in the glass.

1911 Outstanding. "One cold night, in February, 1933," André Simon reminisces, "Francis Berry gave us, at Wimbledon, a wonderful sequence of '11s, with a perfect saddle of mutton and a snipe to help us give them a fair trial."

1915 Good. "It gave every sign of being first class, when young," says Mr. Simon, "but most of the wines of that year hardened instead of becoming mellow with age."

1919 Good. Fruity, stylish.

1920 Good, according to Michael Broadbent. André Simon, however, felt that 1920 was irregular, hence an unsatisfactory year.

WHITE BURGUNDY

"There is a cold partridge on the sideboard, Watson, and a bottle of Montrachet. Let us renew our energies before we make a fresh call upon them."
Mr Sherlock Holmes
The Adventure of the Veiled Lodger

The outstanding vintages of the 19th and early 20th centuries are: 1858, 1864, 1869, 1870, 1874, 1875, 1904, 1906, 1911, 1915, 1919 and 1920.

Some Notes:

1906 Outstanding. A Le Montrachet tasted by Michael Broadbent in 1978 received this note: Pure amber, deep yellow gold, bright and healthy looking; old, smoky, oak-chip, Chardonnay-dry leaves, nutty bouquet, a dry wine, fair body, deep meaty flavour and very long, with firm finish.

1919 Great. A Montrachet tasted by Mr. Broadbent in 1972 "had a deep amber-yellow colour... more bones than flesh, but alive and kicking."

CHAMPAGNE

"Here you are, doggy! Good old Toby! Smell it, Toby, smell it!" He pushed the creosote handkerchief under the dog's nose, while the creature stood with fluffy legs separated, and with a most comical cock of its head, like a connoisseur sniffing the bouquet of a famous vintage.
Mr Sherlock Holmes
The Sign of Four

1857 Great. George Saintsbury's note on the Perrier Jouet 1857, a wine purported to have been part of a parcel shipped to Queen Victoria, reads as follows: "When I bought it in May, 1884, it was 37 years old, of deep amber colour, and nearly but not quite still, though not at all ullaged. It was so majestical that one was inclined to leave it quite alone, and drink it like a slightly sparkling liqueur."

1865 Great.

1868 Excellent.

1870 Very Good. Small harvest.

1874 Magnificent. C. W. Berry: "Excellent wines, fruity, full colour... grand wine, full-bodied."
These wines were of a "darker shade of gold than those of previous vintages, with a faintly pink sheen which made it easy to tell a '74 from any other vintage," says André Simon.

The following poem, entitled 'Ode to Pommery 1874' appeared in *Vanity Fair* magazine in 1894:
>   Farewell, the Pommery Seventy-four!
>   With reverential sips
>   We part and grieve that never more
>   Such wine may pass our lips.

The popular song, 'The Belle of New York', provides another view of the same subject:

>   A case of Pommery '74
>   For any who like to take it.
>   If Pommery says he's got no more
>   He'll jolly well have to make it.

1880 Excellent. Little wine made.

1884 Great. André Simon's tasting note from 1935 describes the wine as "clear as crystal of a beautiful dark gold colour; it had body and power, majesty, in fact, and it was delightful as a great and very real wine, not just 'bubbly', after 50 years of solitary confinement."

1889 Very good. The wines had a distinctive green sheen over the gold. Mr. Simon likened it to the colour of the "Queen Victoria sovereigns one used to come across, before the 'other' war."

1892 Very good. Small yield. The favourite of Edward VII from the time of his coronation to his death in 1910.

1893 Good. George Saintsbury's favourite wine. C. W. Berry deemed it "very good but too ripe."

1899 Superb. Upon tasting Veuve Cliquot in 1920, Berry was moved to write: "What a nose!! Don't gulp it down, take your time over it and ponder on its flavour... Extraordinary. What life!!"

1900 Very good. A panel of wine aficionados headed by André Simon and C. W. Berry concluded that this wine had a fascinating and lingering 'farewell'.

1904 Excellent. "Pommery 1904 ....What a classic!!," exclaims C. W. Berry.

1906 Very good.

1911 Very good. Only a small proportion of the 1911s were shipped before the outbreak of war in August, 1914.

1914 Very good. Champagne was occupied by the Germans.

1915 Good. Picked by prisoners of war and soldiers on leave.

1917 Good. Small harvest.

1920 Very good.

PORT

> When the cloth was cleared Holmes glanced at his watch and filled up three glasses of port. "One bumper," said he, "to the success of our little expedition."
>
> *Sign of Four*

The release of a Vintage Port is determined by a consensus of the leading shippers.

1847 Great. It was about in perfection in 1870 when tasted by George Saintsbury.

1851 Good. Professor Saintsbury said of the vintage: "'51 in all its phases, dry, rich and medium was, I think, such a wine as deserved the famous and pious encomium (slightly altered) that the Almighty might no doubt have caused a better wine to exist, but that he never did."

1858 Good.

1859 Very good.

1863 Great. André Simon, writing in 1945: "my experience of [the 1863s and 1868s] vintages was when they already spent about forty years in bottle [I found] the '63, a lighter wine, did not stand up to the ordeal of time with the sweet smile which '68s did not lose for many years after that."

1868 Great.

1870 Superlative.

1873 Good. "Slightly more highly regarded by the trade at the time," writes Michael Broadbent.

1875 Fine. Low yield due to phylloxera.

1878 Great. André Simon declared: "The '78 was undoubtedly the finest vintage of the decade."

1884 Very good. "The last classic vintage," declared C. W. Berry in 1933.

1887 Good. Queen Victoria's Golden Jubilee vintage. Professor Saintsbury considered it over-rated.

1896 Great.

1897 'Royal Diamond Jubilee' vintage. "In 1959," reminisces Cedric Dickens, "when my father-in-law Colonel Arthur ffrench Blake was 80, I managed to acquire another bottle of Jubilee port from John Davis. The price, l remember well, was only eight pounds ten shillings, and dad sold the empty bottle with its lovely glass medallion for ten pounds. Bless him."

1900 Great. André Simon informs us: "The first two vintage ports of the century, 1900 and 1904, are still good wines, but very different from the old type of vintage port of the 'black-strap' school. They both had charm and good manners, but not the same stamina as their elders."

COPITAS AND ROBBERS

Diverting Trifles Regarding the Wines of Jerez

"...and pulled out a dozen of brown sherry. We cracked off the necks of the bottles, poured the stuff out into tumblers, and were just tossing them off when... there came the roar of muskets... when it was cleared again... Wilson and eight others were wriggling on the top of each other on the floor and the blood, and brown sherry on the table turn me sick now when I think of it.
Mr James Armitage
The Gloria Scott

> "Oct. 4th, rooms 8s., breakfast 2s 6d., cocktail 1s., lunch 2s. 6d., glass sherry, 8d."
>
> "...eightpence for a glass of sherry pointed to one of the most expensive hotels. There are not many hotels in London that charge at that rate."
>
> Mr Sherlock Holmes
> *The Adventure of the Noble Bachelor*

Thirty-three years separate the Old Brown that slakes the thirst of the mutinous prisoners of the *Gloria Scott* from the eightpence glass of Sherry that marks Mr. Francis Hay Moulton out as a swell. During this period popular Sherry styles evolved from heavily sweetened and fortified concoctions to drier, fresher wines.

Gout in the big toe of the Prince Regent made Sherry the fashionable drink of the nineteenth century. He blamed Madeira for his complaint and vociferously vowed to drink Sherry instead. Around this time the pages of the Royal household found their daily bottle of Port replaced by a bottle of Sherry. Quaffed with meals, between meals, before meals; Sherry was to the Englishman of the 1840s and 1850s what a nice cup of tea is today.

The wine sold under generic titles, such as Dinner Sherry (which cost around 2 shillings per bottle), Gold and Old Gold, Brown and Old Brown, Pale Rich and Dark Rich (3 to 4 shillings per bottle) and East India Sherry (5 shillings per bottle).

Michael Broadbent describes Brown sherry as: "deep, rich and brown coloured, as its name implies, the best having a marked amber rim; an altogether different type of bouquet - rich, singed, meaty, sometimes a little raisiny from the use of [Pedro Ximenez] grapes; very sweet, intense thicker in texture."

This style easily masked flaws in the base wine. In 1845 Richard Ford wrote: "In truth, the ruin of

Sherry wines has commenced, from the number of second rate houses that have sprung up, which look to quantity and not quality. Many thousand butts of bad Niebla wine are thus palmed off on the long suffering British public after being well brandied and doctored; thus a conventional notion of Sherry, is formed to the ruin of the real thing."

Be that as it may, demand for the 'doctored' wine continued and supply was always met, this despite the oidium outbreak in the '50s. In 1859 Sherry surpassed Port as the Englishman's favourite tipple.

When Gladstone changed the duty on wines imported into England in 1861 he effectively changed the nature of the Sherry. In 1860 the duty on a butt of Sherry was £31; in 1861 duty on lower alcohol 'still white wine made in the vicinity of Jerez' was reduced to £13. Soon vast quantities of these cheaper, lower alcohol wines were imported and sold as Sherry.

Too light to serve as dessert or after-dinner wines, these 'Gladstone' Sherries were marketed as aperitif wines and drunk on their own or with bitters or gin. Professor Saintsbury advises "he who indulges in them must remember that they are an exception to the general rule that 'Sherry improves in the decanter.' When they are opened, the finer ones especially, must be drunk. I have known a bottle of Tio Pepe become appreciably withered between lunch and dinner."

In 1873 90% of the Sherry produced in Jerez went to Britain. That same year a doctor named Thudichum reported to the Royal Society of Arts: "Sherry wine is never sweet except when it is expressly and intentionally sweetened by makers and exporters... and no Sherry of any claim to quality is ever coloured or sugared, because the maker knows very well that pale, dry wine with the least possible amount of alcohol is far more valuable than the cooked and drugged, coloured, sweet and hot liquids."

By the eighties the taste for the lighter wines was firmly established, although a variety of sweeter styles, including Old Brown and Old Gold, continued to be imported. The huge yields and fine vintages of the 1880's saw the Spaniards through the phylloxera epidemic.

The vogue for Sherry took a dip at the beginning of the twentieth century - 24th June, 1901, to be exact - when Edward VII, a noted wine connoisseur, took a look round the Royal Cellars and came to the daunting conclusion that acquisitions had continued apace during his mother's long widowhood, despite the lady's reduced entertaining. As a result, the cellars were vastly overstocked. The King ordered the sale of a large quantity of wines. The number of Sherries at Christies pre-auction tasting created quite a stir. Word circulated that the King would not drink Sherry. Though untrue, the rumour damaged the wine's reputation.

After the Great War the Old Golds and Old Browns, so beloved by our Victorian ancestors, had lost their widespread appeal. The Sherry Shippers Association desperate to revive the wine's flagging popularity sought to pep up its image by promoting the lighter style sherries as 'more wholesome and cheaper than spirits or cocktails'.

"Sherry," Professor Saintsbury tells us, "may be drunk in glasses small or large, white or coloured, plain or fancy. If it is good it will always be good... The Spaniards, I am told, drink [light styles] in large, tall beakers like our own old fashioned beer glasses and I can strongly recommend the practice."

The Professor was misinformed as to the Spaniards choice in glassware. Although the idea of a beaker of Sherry has a certain appeal, the traditional Spanish Sherry glass, called a copita, is stemmed and has a small bowl that tapers to the rim. It is, in the words of Hugh Johnson, "one of the world's best designed tasting glasses".

Remnants of the old-style blended Sherries remain. Prominent amongst them is Harvey's Bristol Cream. For nearly 200 years a blend called Bristol Milk was popular in England. Sometime in the 1880's (the exact date is unknown) a lady (whose name is also unknown) visited Harvey's cellars and changed the course of Sherry history. She tasted their Bristol Milk and was then invited to taste a lesser known blend. "If that be Milk, then this be Cream," she declared. The Harveys immediately recognized the potential in the name and registered it. More than a hundred years on Bristol Cream remains popular with Sherry drinkers around the world. As you sit quietly sipping your next rich, blended Sherry, give a toast to the unknown lady responsible for the wine in your glass.

CONSUMER DOUROBLES

A Study of Victorian Port Styles

> "One evening, shortly after my arrival, we were sitting over a glass of port after dinner...
> ...Mr. Trevor stood slowly up, fixed his large blue eyes upon me with strange wild stare, and then pitched forward, with his face among the nutshells which strewed the cloth, in a dead faint."
> Mr Sherlock Holmes
> *The Gloria Scott*

When one considers the composition of certain Ports found in English cellars during this period, Mr. Sherlock Holmes could easily have attributed Mr. Trevor's comatose collapse to the effects of a concoction of dried pimentos, elderberry juice, malt, cheap spirits and beetroot wine on a sensitive stomach.

Tampering, or, if you prefer, enhancing, Port is nothing new. In fact, one could say that the venerable, velvety-textured, aristocratic beverage we know today is the result of British merchants making the best of a bad bargain. Port, like Madeira and Sherry, is a British creation, born of necessity.

In 1677 the English established economic sanctions against France and this, naturally discouraged the importation of French wines. To ensure that their citizens would not go thirsty the English made a commercial agreement with the Portuguese. However, that nation's wines were poor stuff compared to claret. Something had to be done to make them more palatable to the British.

A wine agent in Portugal, writing in 1754, sums up the situation:

The English merchants... wished [the wine] to exceed the limits which nature had assigned to it, and that, when drunk, it should feel like liquid fire in the stomach; that it should burn like inflamed gunpowder; that it should have the tint of ink; that it should be like the sugar of Brazil in sweetness, and like the spices of India in aromatic flavour. They began by recommending, by way of secret that it was proper to dash in the fermentation, to give it strength and with elderberries, or the rind of the ripe grape, to give it colour; and, as persons who used the prescription found the wine increased in price...

By the time honoured method of trial and error, Port producers came to realize that if the spirit were added half way through fermentation it would fully integrate with the flavour of the wine. They also came to recognize that to make good Port one must use good spirits.

J. J. Forrester, artist, adventurer, cunning linguist and representative of the firm Offley Forrester and

Co., charged in 1844 that brandy supplied by the Douro Wine Company, who had a monopoly on the spirit used in Port, was "execrable... distilled from figs and raisins of which no other use can be made. They even once tried to make it from locust pods..."

"My countrymen," he said, "do not desire... wine full of brandy; they prefer wines the most pure, and the least inebriative possible." Though of noble mind, Mr. Forrester was somewhat out of touch.

The public still wanted strong and sweet Port, a style that is notoriously easy to imitate. Some wine merchants dispensed with Port all together and manufactured their own 'port-wine'. "Plum and beetroot wine," Mary Aylett tells us in her book, *Country Wines,* "which were once so freely sold as Port, well into the twentieth century, were by some accounts often far less harmful than the liquor they were to replace... the fraud was... seldom discovered... "

It is generally agreed that the Port found in most public houses was 'home-made'. A fact Mr. Holmes must have known when he suggested a stop at the Chequers Inn "where the port used to be above mediocrity and the linen was above reproach." It is quite likely that the Inn's landlady would have been in charge of preparing and maintaining and, quite possible, making both the linen and the liquor.

This is not to say that excellent Vintage Ports were not to be found but a knowledgeable guide was essential. As Henry Vizetelly, one of the first in a series of fine British wine-writers, noted in 1877, "There are almost as many styles of Port wine as shades of ribbon in a haberdasher's shop." There still exists a certain amount of confusion in the minds of many consumers (and wine-shop assistants).

Vintage Port is bottled when young, at around two years. It matures slowly in bottle, retaining its ruby colour for decades, peaking at twenty or more years after vintage.

Late-bottled Vintage Port is kept in barrel and bottled at between six and ten years from vintage. Unlike Vintage Port, it doesn't throws a deposit, as that phase of its development takes place in barrel. It is lighter than Vintage Port and matures after ten or fifteen years.

Tawny, Crusted, White and Ruby Ports are blended with older vintages and matured in barrel.

Tawny Port needs to spend eight years or so in cask. This is an expensive proposition for the vintner. Naturally, there were those who blended Ruby with White Port to create a less expensive product. "A gullible public in England never knew that it wasn't the bargain it seemed," gloats Fritz Hallgarten in his book, *Wine Scandal*.

White Port is made from white grapes and is served as an appertif. It is often dismissed by wine aficionados. However, Professor Saintsbury appreciated it. He considered white Port 'incomparable when good'.

Single Quinta, like Vintage Port, is bottle-matured, but it is made from grapes grown at one quinta [farm], as opposed to a blend from several areas and it is released on the market when ready to drink.

Professor Saintsbury offers this description of a connoisseur's approach to Port: "...a trial of the bouquet; a slow sip; a rather larger and slightly less slow one, and so on; but never a gulp; and during the drinking his face exchanged its usual bluff and almost brusque aspect for the peculiar blandness - a blandness as of Bealah if not of Heaven itself - which good wine gives to worthy countenances."

Ah... had but Mr. Trevor tried this technique.

THE CURIOUS CASE OF THE CAGED CORK

Sparkling Effusions in the Methode Champenoise

"Well, then," cried the other, relapsing in a moment into a bluff joviality, " we are all good friends again and there's an end of the matter." He took a bottle of champagne down from the shelf and twisted out the cork. "See now," he continued, as he filled three high glasses. "Let us drink the quarrelling toast of the lodge."
Mr Jack McGinty
The Valley of Fear

Mr George Leybourne as Champagne Charlie

French Champagne did not soothe the troubled members of Lodge 341. There was no need for them to go that far afield. Rather they indulged in - that great American success story of the nineteenth century - Sparkling Catawba.

Major John Adlum of Maryland is credited with the discovery of the Catawba grape (which he originally named Tokay). "In bringing this grape into public notice," declared Adlum, "I have rendered my country a greater service than I would have done, had I paid off the national debt."

His grand pronouncement was based largely upon the commercial success wrought by Nicholas Longworth of Cincinatti, Ohio (formerly of Newark, New Jersey). In 1825 Mr. Longworth acquired the 'wonder grape' and set about developing its potential. He made America's first 'champagne' in 1842.

A scant twelve yers later, Henry Wadsworth Longfellow, then Professor of English at Harvard, celebrated this strawberry-flavoured, pink-tinged sparkler in his 'Ode to Catawba Wine'.

"Very good in its way
Is the Verzenay
Or the Sillery soft and creamy,
But Catawba wine
Has a taste more divine
More dulcet, delicious and dreamy."

Longworth's Sparkling Catawba sold throughout the United States at the most prestigious establishments. Its reputation was such that Mr. Longworth once indignantly accused some New York Hotels of substituting French Champagne for his American bubbly.

Catawba's fame spread across the pond and in 1858 a writer for *The Illustrated London News* reported that: "the Sparkling Catawba, of the pure, unadulterated juice of the odoriferous Catawba grape, transcends the Champagne of France."

Although the San Francisco firm of Köhler & Frohling began exporting American wines to Europe in 1856, little was imported into England. It is, therefore, unlikely that the inhabitants of Baker Street tasted any New World Sham-pagne. They would have had to content themselves with the French original.

At the start of the nineteenth century 90% of the wines from Champagne were red and most were non-sparkling. Although Dom Perignon, the famous cellar master of the Abbey de Hautvilliers, had experimented with sparkling wine in the early 1700s, the region's winemakers did not embrace the process. It was simply too costly.

What puts the bubbles in the bubbly is the second fermentation that occurs in the bottle. It is started by adding a mixture (dosage) of sugar, yeasts, and wine to still Champagne. If the dosage is improperly measured, too much pressure builds up and the bottle explodes. In 1828, 80% of sparkling Champagne stocks were lost to such explosions. That fact did not daunt the frightfully rich who could afford the thrill of opening a bottle and in 1828 English grandees enjoyed the first running of the Champagne Stakes.

In 1836 François, a clever chemist, invented the sucre-œnometre. With this device the precise amount of sugar present in new wine at the time of bottling could be measured. By 1866 only 15 to 20% of the product was lost through bursting bottles. Improved bottle-making reduced the loss still further. Sparkling Champagne became a viable, if expensive, commercial product.

Champagne of the 1840s and 50s was very sweet. The fashion called for the wine to be frapé, topped with a dash of elderberry juice and served in the famous coupe whose wide shallow bowl is said to have been modelled on the breast of Marie Antoinette.

Professor George Saintsbury felt that there was 'room for real controversy' about glasses for Champagne:

"Its vehicles to the mouth may be classed fourfold: the old tall 'flutes', the modern ballet-girl-skirt inverted, which is supposed to have been one of the marks of the viciousness of the French Second Empire, but which all the world hastened to adopt; tumblers; and nondescript group of large glasses, varying from claret to goblet shape, and sometimes enormous in size. Of these, 1 bar, at once and without appeal, the tumbler... [it] demoralize[s] the wine... the flute is more suitable to sweet champagne the [ballet-girl-skirt inverted] to dry."

The popular taste for sweet, deeply coloured wines remained through the sixties. Most merchants had a great deal of trouble selling drier styles with one notable exception: Ayala's 1865 vintage. The wine became quite popular at the Bullingdon Club in Oxford, where it was the favourite of the Prince of Wales. The Club continued to serve the 1865 vintage until 1933.

In the 60s a good bottle of Champagne sold for around 5 shillings at one's club and for 6 shillings at a bar. In 1869 a case of Pommery 1865 sold for 52 shillings.

With the magnificent 1874 vintage, drier Champagne became the fashion in London. "The man who introduced dry Champagne into this country," wrote H. L. Feuerheerd in 1899 in *The Gentleman's Cellar and Butler's Guide*, "was the late Mr. Hubinet, who, being the agent for Madame Pommery, brought it into the English Market with wonderful energy and success."

"However, the change came...", writes Professor Saintsbury, "the head of the great house of Roederer was, even later, said to have declared that as long as he lived there should be no bowing to the dry Baal in his cellars; and, at any rate in the country, Clicquot was more often still sweet - not to the 'Russe' extent, which was only good for savages or children, but yet not dry."

The price of 1874 Pommery in April, 1882, was 100 shillings per dozen at a wine merchants. Five years later, the same wine fetched 270 shillings at auction. This sensational appreciation created a demand for brand name bubbles. Up 'til then, most Champagne had been shipped to London merchants, who sold it under their own name. With brand consciousness came the first commercial jingles. Vintners subsidised music hall entertainers to perform such ditties as "Champagne Charlie" and "Cliquot, the Wine for Me."*

In the Naughty Nineties a bottle of vintage champers cost a guinea at swank spots such as the Trocadero and around 25 shillings at any of the West End hotel dining rooms. Non-vintage went for from 6 to 10 shillings. Champagne imports into England peaked in 1897 at 9,533,290 bottles.

Without a shade of doubt, it can be stated that Champagne was served at Baker Street. There were so many occasions to celebrate: Doctor Watson's literary successes, his marriage, his return, and one wonders if Mr. Holmes did not occasionally raise a glass in silent toast to *the* woman.

* "Champagne Charlie" was one of George Leybourne's most famous character songs which he sang brandishing a bottle of Moët et Chandon. By subsidising his performances the company secured publicity and a place in the history books as an early commercial sponsor. They provided Leybourne with a retainer and free champagne to lavish on his audiences. Leybourne's great rival was Alfred Vance, whose song "Cliquot" was written in direct competition to "Champagne Charlie", Leybourne responded with a song called "Cool Burgundy Ben" and they went on down the wine list, picking up hand-outs along the way, until Vance arrived at "Beautiful Beer".

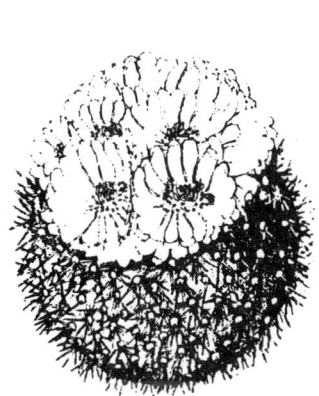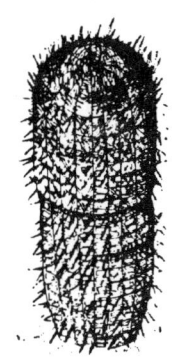

YEA! PURE WINE OF THE GRAPE

The Utahlitarian Approach to Winemaking

> "Better by far that your bones should bleach in this wilderness than you should prove to be that speck of decay which in time corrupts the whole fruit." Mr. Brigham Young
> *The Valley of Fear*

John Ferrier stood in the blistering afternoon heat, weary and parched, from his ordeal in the desert. He raised his arm to block the sun that burned across his face and looked up at the powerfully built young man who was to decide his fate.

Mr. Brigham Young, the leader of The Chosen People of the Angel Moroni, his mind still on the slim brown volume he so often consulted, inspected Ferrier, noticing the man's tough, wiry frame and vigourous constitution. "He's of hearty stock," mused Young, "well able to withstand the hardships of climate and survive harsh terrain. He is adaptable, able to put down roots in new soil and thrive!"

Suddenly the great man's voice rang out, "Will you come with us and abide by our terms?"

"Guess, I'll come on any terms," said Ferrier.

"Take him, give him food and drink, and the child likewise. Let it be your task also to teach him our holy creed. We have delayed long enough. Forward. On, on to Zion."

That said, Young picked up his well-thumbed book and resumed his study.

Ferrier shaded his eyes and squinted at the book's smooth brown cover. He could just make out its title: *A Memoir on the Cultivation of the Vine in America* by Major John Adlum.

"Why, that's the first book on winegrowing published in America," ejaculated Ferrier.

The above scene may well have taken place for Mr. Brigham Young, following the teachings of the founding father of the Mormon religion, Joseph Smith, took a keen interest in winemaking and approved of imbibing. "The original Mormons," Leon Adams tells us in his book, *The Wines of America,* "regularly used wine...for their services when the Church was organized in 1830 at Fayette, New York, for the Book of Mormon is winier than the Bible."

According to the Doctrine and Covenants of the Mormon Church, the Prophet Smith's interest in wine came as a direct edict from an Angel. One day as he was on his way to buy wine for a religious service, the holy apparition appeared and said: "A commandment I give unto you, that you shall not purchase wine neither strong drink of your enemies; wherefore, you shall partake of none except it is made new among you."

When the Mormons moved to Illinois, they chose a site that was ringed by an extensive system of naturally cool caves on which to build the settlement they called "Nauvoo the Beautiful". The wines they made were stored in these caves.

In 1847 after the assassinations of Prophet Smith and his brother Hyrum, Brigham Young led the Mormons on their final journey to the promised land: the broad virgin valley of Utah. During the journey he had grape growing on his mind. "To develop and colonize Utah Territory, one of Brigham Young's chief goals was economic self-sufficiency", writes the Research Librarian for the Church of Jesus Christ of the Latter-Day Saints. "Industrial and agricultural programs were instituted to minimize imports and maximize the amount of items made or grown... Another tack tried was to make or grow items which could be sold to non-Mormon miners and settlers scattered in the region. Two of the items deliberately chosen for the gentile trade were grapes and wine."

Mr. Young issued very specific instructions for winemaking. "First, by lightly pressing make white wine. Then give a heavier pressing and make coloured wine. [The wine should be] properly graded in quality... then stored in oak barrels as far as possible."

Dr. Watson tells us "Young speedily proved himself to be a skilful administrator... In the town streets and squares sprang up by magic. In the country there was draining, hedging and planting..." Dr. Watson fails to mention that Young also made sure that wine presses were located at central places and that vineyards flourished alongside the grain crops.

In the 1850s Mr. Young established Mormon colonies from Salt Lake to southern Utah expressly to plant cotton, sugar-cane and vines and he brought John C. Naegle, a respected œnologist, from Germany to oversee the winemaking enterprise.

To guard against his flock drinking too deeply from the communion cup, Mr. Young ordered special goblets made, 'tumblers that will hold a swallow and no more'.

By 1875 The Church became the single biggest wine and spirit producer in the area. The 554 acres under vine produced around 3000 gallons of wines and brandies each year.

"If my counsel is taken," said Young, "this wine will not be drunk here, but will be exported." His advice wasn't taken.

Many Mormons chose to pay their church tithes with wine. In 1889 Edward H. Snow, clerk of the St. George Tithing Office said, "Our sales during the year do not amount to half of what we are obliged to make up from the grapes that are brought in. We have made at this office alone over 600 gallons this year. We cannot refuse the grapes and I see no way to get rid of it."

By 1890 drunkenness was a worry to the church leaders. The time had come to reinterpret church doctrine. It was decided that the angel who set Prophet Smith on the path to home winemaking had meant 'grape juice' when it had said 'new wine', an easy mistake for a celestial being to make.

The church made a concerted effort to curtail individual winemakers and the Tithing Office at St. George stopped accepting grapes or wine. Not long after the turn of the century winemaking had ceased and wine drinking had become taboo.

Dr. Watson tells us that there was a schism among the Chosen People that caused 'a certain number of malcontents' to leave the Church and become gentiles. Joseph Strangerson and Enoch Drebber were amongst them. The fate of these two gentlemen is well known.

Mr. Strangerson, afraid of trusting his fate to providence, met a bloody end. Mr. Drebber, who failed miserably to learn the value of self-restraint, became a dipsomaniac and died in peculiar circumstances. Had only these unfortunate men retained some of the positive teachings from their Mormon upbringing, how very different would their lives - and deaths - have been.

THE TANTALUS: WHISKY AND BRANDY

Yes, there was a tantalus containing brandy and whisky on the sea-chest.
The Adventure of Black Peter

Drawing by Sydney Paget for *The Adventure of Black Peter*

WHISKY & WHISKEY

The keen eyed among you have no doubt noticed a significant difference in the treatment of the whiskies mentioned in the canon. In England we read of whisky and soda, whisky and water, whisky and a nod at the gasogene. In America, whiskey* (to give it its American spelling) is knocked back neat. This is not merely a difference in national custom. It indicates, in fact, that whisky is whisky and whiskey is quite a different kettle of mash.

Whisky was little known south of the Tweed in the early part of the nineteenth century as the sweet, heavy Highland malts were too flavourful for English palates. The few to find favour in London were the milder Lowland varieties.

Only when experiments with blending began in the mid-1850s did whisky become popular with the Sassenachs. At first the term 'blended whisky' described any mixture of malt whiskies. In time it came to mean a blend of malt whisky and grain whisky. Malt whisky is a distillation of malted barley. Grain whisky is usually distilled from corn to which a small amount of malted barley is added. Blended whisky has a relatively mild taste. The better blends use around 30% grain whisky; cheaper blends up to 70%. In Holmes's time, whisky was aged in old Sherry casks.

* American and Irish whiskey is spelt with an 'e'. Scotch and Canadian lack this 'e'. Whisk(e)y comes from the Irish words *Uisce Beatha* (phonetically isk'ke-ba'ha), which mean Water of Life. It entered the English language via the soldiers of Henry II, who made the first of their several uninvited visits to Ireland in 1170. They developed a taste for the Irish brew, but could never get their tongues round the name. Over the centuries *Uisce Beatha* was Anglicised, first to *Uisce*, then to *Fuisce*, and finally to whiskey.

Blended whiskies filled the gap in the market created by the drastic shortage of French brandy brought about by the phylloxera epidemic. The companies of John Dewar (White Label), James Buchanan (Black & White), James Mackie (White Horse), John Walker, and John Haig all seized this opportunity to make their names in London.

By the 1890s the now booming whisky industry was ripe for fraud. The wily Patterson Brothers¶, originally milk wholesalers, bought cheap grain whisky at under a shilling a gallon, added a minuscule amount of malt whisky, and called it 'Finest Glenlivet'. They sold their creation for 8 shillings and 6 pence a gallon. Their subsequent trial revealed to the public the more despicable elements at the lower end of the whisky trade.

The whiskey the scowsers tossed off could have been Irish whiskey, for during the nineteenth century Irish was a great favourite in the United States. Before the start of prohibition in 1919, more than 400 brands were on the market§. Like Scotch, Irish is based on barley, part of which is malted. The malt for Irish is dried in closed kilns, whilst that for Scotch is dried over open peat fires. Irish is distilled three times in pot stills - no other whisk(e)y is distilled more than

¶ The Pattersons might have fared better had they restricted their creative flair to advertising. The pair arranged for 500 parrots to be trained to say, "Buy Patterson's Whisky". The birds were then distributed to their retail customers. What a concept!

§ Irish was quite popular with the English until blended Scotch was introduced in the 1850s. Elizabeth I was partial to it, as was Sir Walter Raleigh. The trade war with England following the Irish Civil War (1919-21) put the kibosh on the selling of Irish whiskey in the British Empire. This unfortunately coincided with the start of Prohibition (1919-1933) in America.

twice - and it is matured in oak casks for three years by law, but it is usually held in barrel from five to eight years. Irish whiskey has a soft, delicate flavour that deliberately lacks the smokiness associate with Scotch and American whiskies. It is customary to mix Irish half and half with water. This leads me to believe that, although Irish whiskey was available to the scowsers, they chose, instead to knock back neat American whiskey.

American whiskey is made of either unmalted rye or malted wheat or barley on a corn mash. These grains are not dried over peat fires; any smokiness they possess can be attributed to the charred oak barrels in which they are aged. American blends tend to be lighter bodied and milder flavoured than English blends.

Professor Saintsbury describes them thus:

"..the real fact is that the American [whiskies]... are obviously prepared for drinking as liqueurs or cocktails, not for mixing. As such they are not repulsive; they are less good, but not loathsome, as rather sweet toddy; very nasty with cold water; and worse with soda or potash. That they are or were generally drunk 'neat' is, I believe, the fact; and if any rational comparison of the state of America and England in regard to alcoholic liquor were made, this fact would have to be taken into high consideration."

Scotch whisky aficionados wax eloquent on the way a splash of water or soda lifts the peaty notes and releases subtle elements in the bouquet. Most American whiskey fanciers still prefer their tipple neat or 'on the rocks'. As for Irish enthusiasts, well, they aren't much fussed about how you take your whiskey - as long as you enjoy it!

BRANDY

In *Viviana* C. W. Berry said, "Brandy has its invaluable uses. For a thirsty person who cannot digest ales or stouts and who does not care for the manufactured article which emanates from the other side of the Tweed, Brandy is at once refreshing and stimulating."

Brandy is distilled from grape wine. It can be produced in any country, but the best is generally considered to come from the French regions of Cognac and Armagnac.

These areas are separated by some 80 miles. In Cognac the soil is chalky; in the warmer region of Armagnac the soil is sandy.

Cognac is distilled to 70% alcohol whilst Armagnac is distilled to 53%. This lower strength means that the spirit is more flavourful. The barrels for Cognac are made from the porous, low-tannin Limousin oak. Whilst high-tannin black oak is used for Armagnac barrels.

Today to be called Cognac or Armagnac the spirits must come from their designated regions. Until 1905, however, this distinction was irrelevant as most Armagnac was sold to Cognac producers who blended the deeply coloured spirit with young Cognacs to make them seem older and thus fetch higher prices. The borders of Armagnac were not defined until 1909.

The proper way to approach this spirit is exquisitely described by Mr. C. W. Berry:

"...the glass should be held in the right hand between the second and third fingers until such time as the Brandy has taken the warmth of the touch - that is the ideal temperature. While it is being obtained, there need be no waste of time, *au contraire,* for the glass can be gently turned in the hand, this way and that way, and by thus enjoying the fragrance with its stimulating effect the senses will give timely warning to all the members of the body of what a treat there is in store; DON'T HURRY IT, and when the psychological moment does arrive, don't gulp it down, but gently leaning back the head, place the fine rim of the glass on the lower lip, allow a little to escape, but not too much, and as often as not, if one knows how to appreciate the finesse, it will be depicted on the face by the uplifted eyebrow."

In Mr. Holmes's world as documented by Dr. J. H. Watson, brandy only passes one's lips when there is a medicinal need, such as the shock precipitated by the unannounced arrival of an unkempt seaman at teatime. Brandy's health-restoring qualities were greatly respected. *Spiritus vini gallici,* as it is called in the *British Pharmaceutical Codex,* is more fully examined in the chapter on Victorian medicinal imbibing.

THE SPIRIT CASE

With hardly a word spoken, but with a kindly eye,
he waved me to an armchair,
threw across his case of cigars and
indicated a spirit case and a gazogene in the corner.
Scandal in Bohemia

Some spirits have changed a bit since Mr. Holmes's time. What follows is a brief survey of these fuller, richer styles.

GIN

"The craze for drink had seized him again, and he
ordered me to pull up outside a gin palace."
Mr Jefferson Hope
A *Study in Scarlet*

Between a slop-shop and a gin-shop, approached by
a steep flight of steps leading down
to a black gap like the mouth of a cave,
I found the den of which I was in search.
The Man with the Twisted Lip

"I have always been sorry for gin," muses Professor Saintsbury. "First the neglect, and then as usual the hasty action of the legislature brought it into extreme discredit nearly two hundred years ago; and Hogarth, one of the best of artists and fellows, but not precisely of thinkers, made that bad name worse."

There are three basic types of gin: London, Hollands, and Plymouth. London, still a popular style, is made from a fermented mash of grain (usually corn or rye) and malted rye distilled to a nearly tasteless alcohol. This is mixed with flavourings (such as juniper berries, coriander, orris, orange peel, cassia bark, lemon peel, cardamon, angelica and caraway seeds) and distilled again. Distilled water is added to bring the strong alcohol down to 'bottle proof'. The sweetened version of London gin is called Old Tom.

Hollands (Dutch) is distilled only once. The flavourings and grain are distilled together to a much lower proof. Because it needs little dilution, Holland is fuller bodied and has a malty flavour.

Plymouth gin is very flavourful and is said to be distilled with a little sulphuric acid.

British soldiers developed a taste for their pre-battle tot of gin - which they christened 'Dutch Courage' during the Thirty Years War. In the 1860s gin and soda with a slice of lemon was 'the British soldier's delight'.

RUM

"Until about a generation ago," wrote Mr. L. W. Marrison in 1957, "rum was considered to be a rather 'low' drink (from the social point of view) and its consumption was almost wholly confined to sailors." (As astute disciples of Mr Holmes well know.)

In 1891 a Customs order confined the term `rum' to spirits from the West Indies and Demerara. The intention of this decree was to protect unwary buyers from European rums, which were cheap alcohol bases to which rum flavouring had been added.

The rum Mr Holmes hoisted - when disguised as Old Jack Tar - was a dark, flavoured brew, distilled from the juice of sugar-cane. Towday, many rums are distilled from molasses, a by-product of the sugar-cane industry and white rum has been the prevailing taste for the last thirty years or so. However, rum fanciers believe there will be a resurgence of interest in the traditional dark rums. Giles MacDonogh, writing in the April, 1995, issue of *Decanter*, offers some suggestions for those wishing to sip the darker, richer styles:

The best of the dark rums was Rhum Clement from Martinique with its refined orange-biscuit bouquet and long cinnamon taste. Another subtle old rum is the Hors d'Age from Saint James. Again a citrus note creeps in: this is already an after-dinner rum.

In a category that Vincent Osbourne, proprietor of the Brixtonian chain of rum bars and restaurants, calls `real drinks', Mr MacDonogh found:

The 1966 J Bailly Larjas du Carbet, also from Martinique, smelt of butter and liquorice, but the palate revealed a whole range of further delights: cloves, cinnamon, and ginger. The best of the lot was a rare Rhum Vieux de la Guadeloupe, 1948, from the Domaine de Montebello. This was supremely spicey, but with none of the fire or woodiness that affects other rums which have spent more than forty years in the wood.

Though we have wandered rather far from Black Peter's favourite pour, I contend that the journey is worth the while of the serious student of spirits.

CURAÇAO

> "Have you had something to eat? Then join me in a coffee and curaçao."
> Mr Sherlock Holmes to Dr J. H. Watson
> *The Adventure of the Bruce-Partington Plans*

This once respected after dinner liqueur has lost its place at the table and nowadays only occasionally appears at the bar as an ingredient in cocktails.

Curaçao is made from the peel of unripe curaçao oranges. These small bitter fruits from the Dutch West Indies have a strong taste and fragrance.

White Curaçao is a blend of curaçao and other citrus fruit distillates to which sugar syrup is added. It is the base to which colourings are added to make Blue Curaçao (a very old liqueur which used to be called Crême de Ciel), Red Curaçao, and Green Curaçao. Orange Curaçao differs from the others in that it is slightly drier and contains a distillate of bitter oranges and an unsweetened aromatic liquor.

According to the Professor, "Grand Marnier, the recent popular and expensive variant on Curaçao, has never seemed to me quite its equal."

BEHIND BARS

Victorian Mixed Drinks

...I was standing at the Criterion Bar, when someone tapped me on the shoulder, and turning round I recognized young Stamford, who had been a dresser under me at Bart's.
Dr. J. H. Watson
A Study in Scarlet

"There were several bartenders in their shirt sleeves, hard at work mixing drinks for the loungers who fringed the broad, brass-trimmed counter."
The Valley of Fear

Cocktails, in the modern sense, first appeared in the 1800s. They are usually sweet, fairly high in alcohol and served chilled. The older mixed drinks are often drunk hot and are meant to be sipped during friendly chats or when one is in a reflective mood.

What follows are some of the concoctions that were available to Mr. Holmes and his faithful companion.

CANON CONCOCTIONS

HALF AND HALF

"I lent the ostlers a hand in rubbing down their horses, and received in exchange twopence, a glass of half and half, two fills of shag tobacco, and as much information as I could desire about Miss Adler, to say nothing of half a dozen other people in the neighbourhood in whom I was not in the least interested, but whose biographies I was compelled to listen to."
Mr. Sherlock Holmes - A *Scandal in Bohemia*

Lovers of malt liquors in London had their choice of ale, beer and twopenny. Connoisseurs seeking a more subtle flavour than these could offer on their own called for "half and half", half of ale and half of beer or half of ale and half of tuppenny, or half of ale and... well, you get the point.

Half and half has come to mean half of mild ale (I.P.A.) and half of bitter beer.

A FOUR OF GIN HOT

"I was a-strollin' down thinkin' between ourselves how uncommon handy a four of gin hot would be..."
Constable Rance
A Study in Scarlet

From about 1820 to the turn of the century one of the main ways of drinking gin was with hot water. 'A Four' is possibly an abbreviation of the colourful bar-measure, 'four fingers' which is the equivalent of a gill.

WHISKEY PEG

> "There he sat on his veranda, drinking whiskey-pegs and smoking cheroots, while the country was in blaze about him."
>
> Jonathan Small
> *The Sign of Four*

In the tenth century, to keep the citizenry on the straight and narrow, King Edgar ordered that pegs be fastened in drinking vessels at given intervals; anyone who drank beyond these marks at one draught was liable to punishment. Meant as a deterrent they became a provocation.

Peg-tankards contained two quarts, and were divided into eight draughts. They inspired the expressions: "to take him down a peg" and "to put a peg (nail) in one's coffin". In popular parlance any drink of spirits became known as a peg.

Chota is the Bengali word for early. Thus, a chota-peg is an Anglo-Indian slang term for a drink of spirits (usually brandy or whisky) and soda water, which one drinks in the early evening on the verandah, whilst watching the sun set on the British Empire.

PUNCHES & CUPS

BRANDY PUNCH

½ wineglass	Brandy
1 wineglass	Water
1 tablespoon	Raspberry Syrup
2 tablespoon	White Sugar
2 slices of Lemon	
2 slices of Orange	

Serve in a tumbler filled with shaved ice.

PEABODY PUNCH

1 bottle	best Jamaica Rum
6 wineglasses	Cognac
3 wineglasses	Madeira
1 dozen large Limes or 2 dozen small	
1 jar	Guava Jelly
1 pint	Green Tea
Sugar to taste	

Rub sugar on limes until essential oil is diffused into the sugar. Dissolve the sugar in the tea. Then cut the limes, squeeze, and add their juice to the tea. Dissolve the guava jelly in a pint of boiling water. Mix all these until you get the right sweetness; then add the Rum, Cognac, and Madeira. The punch should stand for at least 12 hours. Float a large lump of ice in the punch for an hour before serving, to chill and dilute. The recipe suggests any left-over punch be bottled for future occasion as 'its pleasantness improves with age'.

THE GENERAL

1 bottle of good Claret
1 bottle of Champagne 'Brut'
½ pint Soda-water
½ pint Brandy
½ bottle Orange Curaçao

Chill all the ingredients well before mixing. Mix just before serving. This old army recipe also suggests that 'a tankard of porter may be added to give more body'.

PORT CUP

1 bottle	Ale
1 bottle	Porter
1 glass	Brandy
1 tablespoon	Ginger Syrup
2 tablespoons	Sugar

Mix all the ingredients together, then grate half a nutmeg into it. Put the concoction into the refrigerator for at least half an hour before serving. Just before serving stir in a teaspoonful of Bicarbonate of Soda.

HUNGERFORD PARK

"Hungerford Park is an excellent beverage, and is especially suitable for shooting parties in hot weather," according to John Bickerdyke, writing in 1889.

3 good-flavoured Apples
1 Lemon
3 bottles of Ginger-beer
½ pint of Sherry
2¼ pints of Draught Ale
Loaf sugar
Grated Nutmeg

Cut the apples into slices. Put them into a jug; add the peel and juice of one lemon, a very little grated nutmeg, the ginger-beer, Sherry and ale. Sweeten to taste, stir a little to melt the sugar. Serve well chilled.

PIMM'S CUP

Invented by James Pimm in 1841, Pimm's Cup was commercially marketed in the 1870s. Its recipe is a closely guarded secret known only to the top men of the company, known as the 'Secret Six'. Pimm's may be diluted with ginger ale or fizzy lemonade (Sprite may well be the closest American equivalent). Pimm's is garnished with cucumber sticks, orange slices and sprigs of borage or mint.

COCKLE WARMERS

PORT WINE NEGUS

Put into a tumbler 1 wineglass of Port Wine, 1 teaspoon of Sugar. Grate a little Nutmeg and Lemon Peel on it and add sufficient hot water to make the tumbler one-third full.
(Professor Saintsbury in 1920 lamented that "modern sherries of the drier and less full-bodied kind make negus impossible; with a full golden or brown you may make a fair alternative to the port mixture".)

SHERRY COBBLER

"Sherry Cobbler is indeed a most excellent drink," says Professor Saintsbury, "I was taught to make it as an undergraduate."

Put into a large tumbler 1 tablespoon of Sugar, 2 or 3 slices of Orange, 2 wineglasses of Sherry and fill it with shaved ice. Serve with a straw. As an extra ornament add a few berries in season.
 Cedric Dickens suggests that a tablespoon of Port be added. It "gives the whole a thrilling and inviting appearance," says he.

BISHOP

"I made it myself in my own rooms [at Oxford], for joint consumption with a friend, who, as a matter of fact, actually did become a bishop later," confides Professor Saintsbury.

Bottle of Port
½ Orange
Cloves
Sugar

Pour the Port into a saucepan, add as much water as you think fit. Then add half an orange, plenty of cloves, and sugar to taste. Heat until it begins to steam, light it. "The flames," the Professor says, "will be of an imposingly infernal colour, quite different from the light blue flicker of spirits or of claret mulled. Before it has burned too long pour it into a bowl, and drink it as hot as you like. It is an excellent liquor, and I have found it quite popular with the ladies."

CAUDLE

4 ounces Prepared Groats or Oatmeal
½ pint cold ale
1 quart ale or beer
Allspice
Cinnamon
1 wineglass any Spirit
Sugar to taste

Mix the groats or oatmeal with the half pint of cold ale. Pour this into a saucepan containing a quart of boiling ale, or beer. Add a few whole allspice, and a little cinnamon. Stir the caudle over a low heat for about half an hour, and then strain it into a basin or jug. Add a glass of any kind of spirits and sugar.

FLIP

1 quart Strong Ale
2 Lumps of Sugar
Lemon Rind
Cinnamon
1 glass cold Ale
6-8 Eggs
Powdered Sugar
Grated Nutmeg

Place the Strong Ale in a saucepan with the lumps of sugar which have been rubbed with lemon rind and cinnamon. Take the mixture off the fire when boiling and add one glass of cold ale. Have already in a jug the yolks of six or eight eggs well beaten up with powdered sugar and grated nutmeg. Pour the hot ale from the saucepan on to the eggs, stirring them whilst so doing. Have another jug at hand and pour the mixture as swiftly as possible from one vessel to the other until a white froth appears. One or two wine glasses of gin or rum are often added.

SHANDY GAFF

1 pint Bitter Beer
1 bottle old-fashioned Ginger-beer

Mix together and imbibe only on the hottest summer days, after rowing.

TEWAHDIDDLE

1 pint of Beer
1 tablespoon Brandy
1 teaspoon Brown Sugar

Mix all ingredients together and garnish with a little grated nutmeg or ginger, and a roll of very thinly-cut lemon peel.

DOG'S NOSE

(This has been described as a 'policeman's drink when on duty on cold nights'.)

1 tablespoon Brown Sugar
1 pint warmed Beer or Guinness
1 shot of Gin

Mix ingredients. Garnish with nutmeg. Drink warm.

FANCY BAR-ROOM DRINKS

Note: The jigger measure in the days these recipes were developed was 2 ounces. It has shrunk to 1½ ounces in modern times. A pony is 1 fluid ounce. A wineglass is a shade more than 2 fluid ounces. A dash is a teaspoon.

BURNT BRANDY AND PEACH

1 wineglass of Brandy
½ tablespoon of Sugar
Several slices of dried peach

Pour the brandy and the sugar into a saucer and set fire to them. When the flame has extinguished pour the liquid into a small bar glass containing the dried peach slices.

FANCY BRANDY

1 Jigger fine Brandy
1 Dash Orange Bitters
2 Dashes Angostura Bitters
3 Dashes Maraschino

Mix ingredients. Moisten rim of glass with piece of Lemon and dip in Powdered Sugar.

BRANDY, WHISKY OR GIN SMASH

½ tablespoon of Sugar
1 tablespoon of Water
2 sprigs of Mint
1 slice of Orange
1 wineglass of Brandy, Whisky or Gin

Mix ingredients and serve in a small bar glass two-thirds filled with shaved ice.

FRENCH POUSSE CAFE

Equal parts Brandy, Kirchwasser and Curaçao Liqueur.
Serve in small wineglasses.

DUNHILL

1 measure of gin
½ measure Orange Curaçao
½ measure Dry Vermouth
½ measure Amontillado Sherry
1 dash Anisette

Shake well with ice, strain into a cocktail glass. Decorate with a twist of Orange peel.

ROB ROY

1 Measure of Scotch
3 dashes Angostura Bitters
1 Sugar Cube

Stir the ingredients together well in a tumbler until the Sugar dissolves completely and then add two or three cubes of ice which should be just covered with liquor.

JERSEY COCKTAIL (Could this have been a tribute to Mrs. Godfrey Norton?)

Mix a teaspoonful each of Sugar and Cocktail Bitters with a small bar tumbler filled with Cider. Decorate with a piece of Lemon Peel.

BLACK VELVET

¼ pint Guinness (preferably draught)
¼ pint very dry Champagne

Into a glass tankard pour the Guinness followed by the Champagne.

CHAMPAGNE COCKTAIL

Equal (small) parts of Brandy, Curaçao, Maraschino, and Grand Marnier
1 Lump of Sugar sprinkled with Bitters
Champagne

Place the sugar lump in the bottom of a Champagne coupe and shake on 2 dashes of Angostura bitters. Add the Brandy and the Liqueurs. Fill the glass with Champagne.

CLASSIC CHAMPAGNE COCKTAIL

1 Lump of Sugar sprinkled with Bitters
1 measure of Brandy
Champagne

Place sugar lump into the bottom a Champagne flute and shake on 2 dashes of Angostura bitters. Add a measure of Brandy and fill with Champagne. Sometimes decorated with a slice of Orange.

COLLINS

The JOHN COLLINS, named for a nineteenth century London barman, was made with "Holland Gin". The TOM COLLINS was made with "Old Tom", a sweet London gin.

1 measure of Gin
Juice of 1 Lemon
1 teaspoon Sugar
1 dash Angostura Bitters
Soda for topping up

Place all the ingredients except the soda into a highball glass and mix. Add two or three ice cubes and then top up with soda. Decorate with a slice of Lemon.

OLD TOM COCKTAIL

1 wineglass of Old Tom Gin
3 Dashes Gum Syrup
2 Dashes Angostura Bitters
2 Dashes Curaçao
1 Twisted Lemon Peel

Place all the ingredients except the soda into a highball glass and mix. Decorate with twisted Lemon peel.

MARTINEZ COCKTAIL

This is the precursor of the Martini. Some say is was invented in San Francisco by the famous barman, Dr. Jerry Thomas, at around the time Mr. Francis Hay Moulton and his lovely fiancée, Miss Hatty Doran, were in town. Others say it is an English invention, named for the Martini Rifle used in India.
Use small bar glass.

1 dash of Bitters
2 dashes of Maraschino
1 wineglass of Vermouth (Sweet Italian Vermouth)
2 small lumps of ice
1 ounce of Old Tom Gin (A Sweet Gin)

Shake up thoroughly and strain into a large cocktail glass. Put a quarter of a slice of Lemon in the glass, and serve. If the guest prefers it very sweet, add two dashes of gum syrup.

HAIR OF THE DOG

2 measure Scotch Whisky
1½ measure Double Cream
1 measure Clear Honey

Shake the ingredients well with crushed ice.

A STUDY IN CLARET

What Drives a Wine Merchant to Crime?

A wine merchant's lot can be a very fortunate one, offering as it does the joy of tasting great vintages, the gratification of satisfying a discriminating clientele and, if one's firm has sufficient sales, the pleasure of being wooed and fêted by wine and spirit producers. There is, however, a dark side to this existence that emerges when an ignoble person enters this noble profession.

Two wine merchants are mentioned in the canon: the enigmatic Mr. Vamberry whose adventures are not revealed by Dr. Watson and Mr. James Windibank, who appears in A *Case of Identity*. It is the latter gentleman's behaviour which will serve to illustrate what drives some vintners to crime.

Let us first examine the characteristics of an honourable supplier of wine. He has a winning disposition and a thorough understanding of the laws regulating his trade. He is also frequently an epicure, whose generous spirit spills over to include all within decanter distance. He is, all in all, the most charming of people.

The ideal wine merchant's daily dealings with the new and old rich develop in him an acute awareness of social distinctions. A well balanced individual maintains proper etiquette, his rage unengaged, when confronted with the occasional ill-mannered client who persists in treating the skilled professional as if he were a skivvy. Nor is he phased by the time-honoured custom of noble families of ignoring troublesome bills. Until quite recently in England, the purveyor of wine came low on the pecking order of debts to be settled. Mr. C. W. Berry, writing in 1920, tells of one 'old and friendly client' who owed a considerable sum for several years. He repeatedly promised to pay but somehow never got around to it. Finally a warrant was served on him which promptly brought this reply:

> Gentlemen,
> Your letter with enclosure has given me a terrible shock, so much so that I shall require help to overcome it; therefore I beg you to send me six dozen of the best burgundy at once. I return the offending document, to which you are at liberty to add the cost of the wine and then do your damnedest.

Whilst Mr. Berry makes light of such incidents, treatment of this kind might indeed sour a less self-possessed soul such as James Windibank.

The flaws already existing in Mr. Windibank's character are easily exploited when he enters the wine trade.

Far from upholding the virtues of the ideal, this

gentleman is, rather, an example of the dodgy wine merchant. He is aware of the law only so that he may stay poised on the brink of its boundaries. "It's not actionable," is his cry. He applies his charm to such nefarious ends as donning false beard and goggles in order to lead his short-sighted step-daughter, the lovely Miss Mary Sutherland, down the garden path.

By no stretch of the imagination can Mr. Windibank be considered a true epicure, for he lacks generosity and without generosity good cheer and enjoyment degenerate into decadence and carnality. He is both a mountebank and a miser: he begrudges Miss Sutherland the very necessities of a young woman's existence - a new frock, an evening out, a visit to a consulting detective. This meanness of spirit rubs rough against the grain of an epicure.

Miss Sutherland tells us that Windibank "was very superior, being a traveller in wines". Indeed, in the employ of Westhouse & Marbank, the great claret importers of Fenchurch Street, he might well have been treated with princely deference by fawning producers and negotiants in Bordeaux. Upon his return to London he would again become just another salesman. From *lampoies a la Bordelaise* deliciously enhanced by fine claret he would once again be washing down his eel pie with some dubious petite château. His resentment shows.

"I am afraid I am a little late, but I am not my own master, you know," he says with ill grace upon arriving at his meeting with Mr. Sherlock Holmes.

Nursing intimations of deep seated insecurity and sentiments of social inferiority, Windibank is easily seduced by the grandiose dreams and fraudulent schemes that thrive in the fertile soil of his trade; for any business that deals with great sums of money and depends upon discriminating judgment provides many an opportunity for a weak man to stumble and for a cad to tumble headlong into the mighty vortex of crime, a spiralling decline that can only end at the gallows.

A NOTE ON MEMBERS OF THE BREWING TRADE

Wine drinking bears with it the dangers of snobbery and social pretention whereas the image associated with beer is one of down-to-earth good cheer and camaraderie. As direct producers of their particular alcoholic beverage rather than mere middlemen brewers and hop dealers are at liberty to lavish hospitality upon all and sundry. Those who appear in the canon evince this characterization. Mr. Melville, the retired brewer in *The Adventure of Wisteria Lodge,* invites to share the bounty of his table a chap he, seemingly, knows nothing about, whilst Mr. Monro, the hop merchant in *The Yellow Face,* kindly accepts the child of his wife's first marriage with open arms and an open heart.

A NOTE ON CHÂTEAU KIRWAN

Château Kirwan, a classed growth in Bordeaux, takes its name from the English family who founded it in the fifteenth century. Alas, the seed of the ancestors of the unfortunate coachman, William Kirwan, who met his end in *The Reigate Puzzle,* fell on the shady side of the family tree and did not flourish as did that of his expatriate relations.

WHAT WAS IN THE CELLAR BESIDES MRS TOLLER?

"Is there a cellar with a good strong lock?"
"Yes, the wine cellar."
Mr Sherlock Holmes to Miss Violet Hunter
The Adventure of the Copper Beeches

In the Victorian period any man with a few hundred pounds a year maintained at least a modest store of wines. Until the Kaiser's War all large country houses had decent cellars and London middle-class dwellings were certainly equipped with them until the mid-1800s. From that time on, metropolitan builders gave scant importance to wine storage and the householder was reduced to keeping his alcoholic beverages in a cupboard under the stairs or in a small closet. Country residences continued to offer more luxurious accommodation for wines, spirits and the occasional housekeeper, as Mrs. Toller would attest.

Let us join that distressed lady as she pounds against the locked door of the Copper Beeches cellar. Although her expenditure of energy admirably serves to raise her body temperature and thus ward off the cold - a proper cellar is kept at between 50 and 55 degrees Fahrenheit - had she been a privileged member of The Adventuresses of Sherlock Holmes she would have spared her knuckles and found a less strenuous way to encourage a warming glow.

The floor and walls of the multi-roomed cellar are made of brick or stone and have built-in vaulted bins that hold 25 dozen bottles (the content of a hogshead). These may be augmented by wire bins. Every effort is taken to avoid draughts and extreme fluctuations in temperature.

The major portion of the wine in the cellar comes from France. Rupert Croft-Cooke, writing in 1966, reveals the Englishman's prejudices:

> The truth is fairly well acknowledged - only two countries, France and Germany, produce great table wines, and only two, Spain and Portugal (with its island Madeira), produces great fortified wines. All others are 'the rest', though they may in time become of more importance.

To the English, France meant Bordeaux, Burgundy and Champagne. Before 1914 most wines shipped to the United Kingdom were bottled and labelled by the merchant selling them. These wines tended to be sold by generic names or simply by region. Burgundies labelled Beaune and Pommard have always been particularly popular in the United Kingdom, due in large part to their easily pronounceable names.

One of the exceptions to generic labelling was Classified Growth claret. These wines had grand reputations to protect and every English cellar had a stock of them along with lesser *cru bourgeois*.

Champagne is kept in the driest room of the cellar, as dampness can affect the wire enclosures that hold the corks firm against the pressure of the Carbon Dioxide that builds up inside the bottle. Undoubtedly, a good selection of both sweet and dry styles of this wine are to be found in the cellar. (Rosé Champagne became popular in England when King Edward VII took a fancy to it.)

The cellar maintains a few bottles of such popular liqueurs as Chartreuse (flavoured with herbs found in the Dauphine valley), Curaçao (17 bottles of this liqueur were in the cellar of Charles Dickens when it was inventoried in 1870), Maraschino (from bitter cherries and almonds), Kummel (flavoured with caraway seeds and said to be a favourite of Queen Victoria), Ratafia (a favourite in the 19th century made from cherry and peach kernels) and Crême de Menthe (formerly made only in France from mint grown in England).

Shelves for bottled beer, gin and arrack (a favourite Victorian spirit often used as a base for punch) line one wall. Irish whiskey, brandy and rum (for punch) are kept in bottle as well as cask.

There are at least two barrels of beer: one set aside for the benefit of the domestics, the other intended for the gentry.

The quintessentially British libations, cider and perry, also spent time in barrel, as did, obviously, Scotch whisky.

Professor Saintsbury advises one to "acquire a cask [of whisky] of whatever size your purse and your cellar will admit, from a butt to an 'octave' (14 gallons) or an 'anker' (10 gallons) or even less, fill it up with good and drinkable whisky from six to eight years old. Stand it up on end, tap it half way down or even a little higher, and, when you get to or near the tap, fill it up again with whisky fit to drink, but not too old."

Many cellars had casks of Madeira and Sherry and every cellar had a barrel or two of Port. The Professor tells us that "an ordinary family would consume a bottle [of Port] often, if not daily" and every Victorian gentleman laid down a pipe of Port (522.5 litres) upon the birth of a son.

Vintage Port, just ready to bottle, could be bought quite cheaply. "For nearly a hundred years before the war," says the Professor, "the price averaged some thirty to six-and-thirty shillings a dozen; it seldom or never plays the tricks that claret, in growing up, will sometimes do; it will treble its value in twenty or five and twenty years, and when it is matured, if you want to get rid of it, it will fetch full price."

Decanting is done in the cellar so as to avoid disturbing the sediment in the bottle. A large decanting table stands squarely in the centre of the main room. A wooden bench is next to it. On the table are candles and matches, a decanting vessel, a cloth for wiping the lip of the bottle, a silver bell-shaped funnel with strainer, a cellar-book and pen, a glass or two, and, of course, a corkscrew.

"Well!" as Professor Saintsbury so merrily points out, "a cellar is an interesting place to fill, to contemplate when filled, and to empty in the proper way": advice which our imprisoned Adventuress would undoubtedly have no hesitation in heeding.

HIS LAST GLASS

Remedies for Rheumatism

> And yet I live and keep bees
> upon the Sussex Downs.
> Mr. Sherlock Holmes
> *His Last Bow*

In her fine book, A *Compound of Excelsior,* Holmesian luminary and scholar, Miss Susan Rice, neatly demonstrates that Mr. Holmes was more than an avid apiarist. He was, she explains, examining the curative properties of bee venom in search of a treatment for his rheumatism. I should like to suggest that Mr. Holmes's enquiries took him beyond the angry bee's sting and led him to explore the medicinal merits of monoflora honey as it is used in alcoholic beverages.

A monoflora honey is one derived from a single source of pollen. Noted herbalists, Eraclio Fiorani and Roberto Fedecostante in their book, *Vini Medicinali,* suggest that the plants on which bees feed impart their own medicinal properties to the honey. Mr. Holmes, therefore, would have been keenly interested in feeding his bees on Thyme.

Since antiquity both *Thymus serpyllum* and *Thymus vulgaris* have been used to treat rheumatic pains. The herb benefits sufferers by aiding in the elimination of uric acid. Thyme can also be applied locally to easy joint pains. The late nineteenth and early twentieth century saw a flurry of activity amongst scientists studying the medicinal uses of this herb: in 1887 the French physician, Dr. Chamberland (the elder), proved the bactericidal action of thyme essence; in 1889 Drs. Caeac and Meunier demonstrated its effect on the typhus and glanders bacilli; Dr. Miquel discovered the bactericidal power of vapours of thyme in 1894; during the Great War applications of aromatic essences, including thyme, were used in civilian and military hospitals and in the 1920s French scientists Courmont, Morel and Bay studied its effect on tuberculosis bacilli.

Thyme's effects are powerful and it is usually administered in a much diluted state in an alcohol solution. The solutions chosen by Mr. Holmes for this purpose were quite likely: mead, metheglin and pigment.

Mead, fermented honey wine, was a popular home-brew in Britain until the late eighteenth century. The wine's decline can be traced to the importation of cheap cane and beet sugar which replaced honey as the common sweetening agent. Soon mead making became the domain of the beekeeper.

Virgin honey - that which is drained from the comb without pressing - is honey in its purest form and is crucial to the making of fine mead. Honey musts are quite high in saccharine and should be allowed to ferment to dryness. Proper mead is, therefore, highly alcoholic and is oft described as fiery. It takes considerable time to mature; a year is the very minimum. Some makers advise the wine be left for as long as seven years.

Whilst Mr. Holmes patiently waited for his mead to develop he surely must have studied formulæ for metheglin, the very name of which is derived from the Welsh word for medicine.

Metheglin is mead flavoured with herbs and spices. The Greeks thought it a universal panacea. Hippocrates recommended it for all cases of sickness that had no tendency toward delirium. This is a sound caution as metheglin is capable of producing quite a nice little delirium all by itself if indulged in too freely.

A nineteenth century metheglin recipe calls for the addition of rosemary, cloves, ginger and a sprig of sweetbriar. This version is said to resemble Tokay. As the herbal constituents of this beverage are added during fermentation, metheglin takes even longer than mead to achieve a total integration of flavours.

Pigments have a long history of providing medicinal comfort. They are a concoction of wine, honey, herbs and spices and are usually served hot. Mr. Holmes must have concocted a few of these whilst his metheglin matured.

The most famous pigment is Hippocras, made with white wine. Bishop is made with red wine, ginger, cloves, honey, hot water and a roasted lemon or orange. Cardinal uses claret as its base but in other respects it is the same as Bishop. Higher up on the clerical scale is Pope. This drink takes no chances and insures its medicinal potency by using (Hungarian) Tokay or Champagne as its base-wine.

Mr. Holmes could hardly have ignored the body of evidence that supports the medicinal claims of these honeyed beverages. Alcohol, honey and thyme all possess medicinal substances that have excited the attention of scientists from ancient times.

In addition, the process of winemaking is peculiarly suited to Mr. Holmes interests and - more importantly - temperament. It allows him to indulge his enthusiasm for science by pursuing œnological studies whilst allowing for "the swings of his nature [that] took him from extreme languor to devouring energy". These aspects are mirror images of the tumultuous frenzy of fermentation that is followed by the long and tranquil process of maturation.

Can you not see him as he sits in the cool, dry cellar his violin tucked under his chin? Can you not hear the low, dreamy melody with which he settles his mind and his musts? Can you not smell the sharp tang of scientific research in the air?

Mr Ellie Norwood as Sherlock Holmes in *The Return of Sherlock Holmes* (192:

WHAT THE DOCTOR ORDERED

1. Victorian Medical Imbibing

1. If you felt faint which would you prefer your doctor to prescribe?
    a. a tablespoon of sal volatile
    b. a cup of Champagne
2. If you were given surprising news that sent you into a state of shock which would you prefer your doctor to administer?
    a. an injection of 10cc.'s dextrose
    b. a snifter of brandy

3. If your thigh-high wooden leg were stuck in the mud of a riverbank, and you were then lassoed and pulled into a waiting launch, which could you rather your rescuer/captor offer?

    a. a good sized bath towel and perhaps an aerosol can of lemon Pledge

    b. a cigar and a pull from a handy pocket flask

If you did, indeed, answer b, you are truly sons and daughters of the Victorian era. For beer, wine and spirits were an essential part of the professional and domestic pharmacopœia of that time. Doctor J. H. Watson would have prescribed them freely.

Most alcoholic beverages were made at home until well into the nineteenth century. Beer was brewed in the kitchens of every humble cottage and the still-rooms of each venerable pile. As fruits and flowers of the countryside came into season, wines were made. The healing properties of each and every sprig of greenery, tumescent berry and thicket thorn was recognized and esteemed.

Blackberry wine eased the discomfort of fretting and of eating sores, parsley wine soothed the rheumatic; marigold strengthened the weak of heart; parsnip wine served as a mild laxative and diuretic. Those with bronchial troubles sipped elderflower wine. Whilst elderberry wine was a panacea for anything that could ail a body, including curing the symptoms of the common cold. Queen Victoria and her adored Albert fancied tonic Birch wine and copious quantities were made and consumed during their stays at Balmoral.

Most of these wines need a few months of cellaring to reach a kind of drinkability. Beer on the other hand is nigh on ready a few days after bottling. Spruce beer, made from tree sap, purified the blood something splendid and tackled all internal ailments, particularly gastric ulcers. It retained its popularity with home brews up until the Great War.

Nettles provided the source for many a stimulating restorative. Nettle beer is high in Vitamin C and was considered a good treatment for rheumatism and asthma as well as boosting declining vitality.

The Victorians considered Porter, a strong beer invented in the eighteenth century, to be the most nourishing of all alcoholic beverages. Even genteel ladies knocked back a good deal of the stuff - to fortify the blood, you understand. This is not such a farfetched idea, for even a weak beer provides around a tenth of the daily requirements of calcium and phosphorous and around a fifth of the B vitamins.

Public perception of the tonic properties of strong beer was such that around the turn of the century every bottle of Guinness Foreign Export Stout carried the following testimonial from Sir Charles Cameron, the Vice President of the Royal College of Surgeons, Ireland.

> "I have analyzed a specimen... [and find] it possesses only in the highest degree the good qualities of Dublin Export Stout and has evidently been brewed from the very best materials. It contains nearly seven percent of solid matter in solution and is, therefore, a food as well as a stimulant and tonic."

Another contemporary of Dr. Watson's found an intriguing medicinal use for Guinness. He relates his methods as follows:

> As I am an Ophthalmic Surgeon I have not much occasion to prescribe Guinness as a general tonic although I am well aware of its tonic properties, but there is however one condition in which unless I am dealing with a teetotaller I prescribe Guinness as a routine. This is the condition of Tobacco amblyopia which is some-

times found in pipesmokers who use strong tobacco and who smoke up to six or seven ozs. a week without cleaning their pipe. As the only method of curing this condition is complete abstinence from tobacco for a few months at least, the patients become very upset. But I find that by making them spend the equivalent amount of money on Guinness daily as they would on tobacco they become much more resigned to stop smoking.

Victorians practising preventative medicine started the day with a shot of 'bitters', also called 'bitter wine'. Based on wormwood, the herb used to flavour absinth, these mixtures were said to strengthen ones constitution.

John Dunlop, in his *Artificial and Compulsory Drinking Usage of the United Kingdom*, published in 1844, tells us that the great majority of middle and upper-middle class ladies in Scotland and England drank healths in the morning with brandied wine. Mr Dunlop excludes from this practice ladies of the very highest rank; which he defines (in masculine terms, of course) as "nobility, country gentlemen of very large fortune, judges, rich and dignified clergy and professional men of great wealth and eminence." This practice of a morning shot continued among middle-class English ladies until well into the 1860's. The practice held on quite a bit longer in Scotland.

Among the very wealthy classes fine wines were used to good effect. If one felt faint one was admonished to sit down and have a cup of Champagne. André Simon, writing in 1945, continues to extol the virtues of this wine: "Champagne is the finest pick-me-up, the most helpful of all wines in cases of debility, digestive troubles, convalescent or old age, but its merciful and helpful mission is denied by our legislators to all who need it most, the poor among us." Hear! Hear!

A glass of claret was just the ticket if one were feeling a bit run down. Mr. Holmes availed himself of this prescription after his three day fast. "'I never needed it more,' said Holmes as he refreshed himself with a glass of claret and biscuits in the intervals of his toilet."

To Port "we owe...the life of that great statesman, William Pitt, first Earl of Chatham," explains C. W. Berry. "...[Pitt] was so ill at about the age of fifteen that he had to give up his studies at Cambridge (he matriculated at fourteen) and return home. Here he was placed under the care of Dr. Addington, who recommended a very free use of Port Wine. This had the desired effect, and at the age of eighteen his health was restored."

The most famous medicinal wine is Hungarian Tokay Essence. In his book, *Viniana*, Mr. Berry relates a number of remarkable cases in which the wine restored health when all hope had been abandoned. The Royal family evidently kept a store of the wine just in case - as Mr. Berry relates:

"In recent years, it has been borne in upon me in a very convincing manner that this wine - the Essence of Tokay has a most wonderful effect in cases of extreme illness... When our good King Edward VII, bless his memory, was taken suddenly ill, and the coronation had to be postponed, I was at the office... a messenger arrived from the Palace inquiring if we had any Tokay Essence, as their small stock was at Windsor... Whether any Tokay... was used or not I will not pretend to say; but the inference is that it would not have been asked for had it not been either required or considered advisable to have in readiness in case of emergencies."

In 1860 Mr. William Ewart Gladstone, the

Chancellor of the Exchequer, changed the drinking habits of the nation when he reduced the duties on light or natural wines to one shilling per gallon. Within two years the amount of French wines imported into Great Britain tripled. By 1873 eight times as much French wines flowed down the throats of grateful Britons. Accustomed to hearty fortified wines some citizens boosted these lighter wines with a shot of bitters or gin.

Gladstone's policies also opened up the wine trade to grocers, haberdashers, anyone with the price of a license. These new wine purveyors often had great enthusiasm but little professional knowledge. Prior to 1860 wine merchants had been a superior lot, accustomed to dealing with only the best sort of people and the best sort of wine. Claret and other fine French wines had been beyond the means of all but the very wealthy.

Following Gladstone's pronouncement in 1860, Dr. Robert Druitt published a highly popular discourse, entitled [a] *Report on the Cheap wines of France, Italy, Austria, Greece and Hungary*. The doctor assures us, "I have bought and drunk not for gratification of the palate, but for real professional study, specimens of most of the varieties of wines available."

The results of his studies are edifying. He finds claret beneficial "particularly for children, for literary persons, and for all those occupations chiefly carried on indoors, and which use the brain more than the muscles."

By the '80s doctors were of two minds about the benefits of wine. Whilst many continued to extol its merits, other pronounced wine to be a gouty, sub-acid, liquid and instead recommended Whisky. The Queen appreciated the medicinal virtues of a daily dram and used to enjoy one in her tea. On 12th

September, 1848, Victoria, the Prince Consort and family visited the Lochnagar distillery only a mile from Balmoral. The Queen was so pleased with the sample she tried that she granted the distillery a royal warrant. It has thenceforward been known as Royal Lochnagar.

Perhaps the most widely known medicinal use of whisky is the Hot Toddy. It first appeared in literature in the seventeenth century. A number of recipes have evolved, some elaborate, calling for a dash of Madeira or a splash of angostura. The definitive Toddy recipe may well be that of Matthew Gloag, of Matthew Gloag and Son, Limited, Perth: "...when one is struck with the 'flu, one should retire to bed with a large whisky, a tablespoon of honey and the juice of a lemon diluted with a spot of boiling water. Upon retiring, one should place a hat at the foot of the bed and continue sipping until two hats are seen. One should wake up the next morning ready to take on the gravest problems."

Spirits, such as brandy and whisky, had well served doctors and dentists as an anaesthetic during tooth extractions and surgery prior to the discovery of ether in 1846 and continued to be used in that capacity when supplies of the gas ran low. A good stiff drink was regularly administered to post-operative patients.

Spirits were used as antiseptics and, of course, many a shock victim had copious quantities poured down his throat. The idea of medicinal spirits is so great that Allied Distillers still make an export brand whisky called Doctors Special.

Brandy was a remedy of which Dr. Watson and Mr. Holmes readily availed themselves. Even with an injured arm the doctor had no problems reaching for the decanter on the sideboard. Nor did Mr. Holmes travel far without his handy pocket flask.

"Drink this," Dr. Watson advises Mr. Victor

Hathersley, as blood drips from the unfortunate engineer's bandaged hand. "Keep your strength up with a little stimulant," Mr. Holmes encourages the fellow. A drop of brandy brought colour back to the cheeks of Mr. Scott Eccles and Thorneycroft Huxstable, MA, PhD, etc. Whilst it worked a wondrous change in Ian Murdock. With the aid of ammonia and brandy Dr. Watson drew Mr. Melas back from that 'dark valley in which all paths must meet'. Brandy served to steady the palpitating hearts of Mr. Percy Phelps and Mr. James Ryder who were both quite staggered by Mr. Holmes's dramatic flourishes.

Mr. Holmes himself, a bit shaken from his tussle with the Cunninghams, took a tot. And it was with the tingling taste of Mr. Holmes's brandy on his lips that Dr. Watson came to after his fainting fit.

In 1900 Sir William Osler, Regius Professor of Medicine at Oxford and possibly the most brilliant physician of his day, called alcohol 'our most valuable medicinal agent' and 'the milk of old age'. At that time all hospitals stocked brandy, beer and whisky.

These were prescribed for just about any ailment and administered to all ages: babies slurped a mixture of spirits and water to encourage them to sleep, young children sipped tasty blackberry brandy for stomach aches, nursing mothers took a healthy glass of vitamin rich Guinness, and the old tossed back beer to ease the pain of arthritis, Sherry to improve the appetite, and brandy to send them off to a peaceful, restoring sleep.

Sherry, Guinness, sweet stout and brandy are still given on geriatric wards in the United Kingdom. Professor Oliver James, Great Britain's leading specialist in treating the aged, believes that a drink not only helps the elderly drift off to sleep but also prevents heart attacks and strokes. The professor affirms that, "A little tot at bedtime works wonders."

In maternity hospitals in the United Kingdom (and, of course, France) pregnant women suffering from anaemia are prescribed a glass of iron rich red wine per day to raise their hæmoglobin and nursing mothers are still encouraged to take a little Guinness or stout to stimulate appetite.

Sadly, the Champagne cure for faintness has fallen from favour and scientists have found that a short sharp shot of brandy is not really what a body needs when suffering from shock.

However, many of the Victorian medicinal imbibing practices have merit and we could all not only improve our health but also get a more intimate view of the pharmacological milieu in which Dr. Watson practised by taking a medicinal nip now and then. It is, indeed, our duty as Holmesians to pursue these researches with vigour.

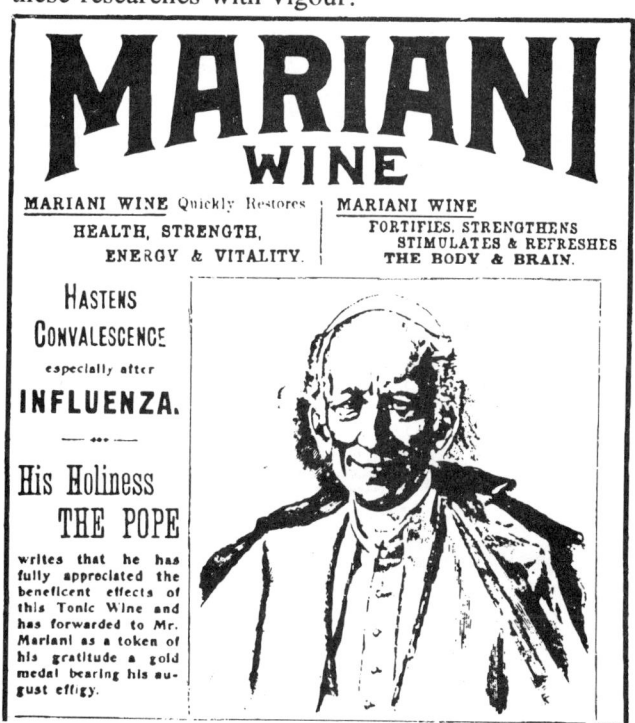

THE SCIENCE OF DEGUSTATION

> There are seventy-five perfumes, which it is very necessary that a criminal expert should be able to distinguish from each other, and cases have more than once within my own experience depended upon their prompt recognition.
> Mr. Sherlock Holmes
> *The Hound of the Baskervilles*

> ...we all know you are a connoisseur of crime...
> Mr. Athelney Jones
> *The Sign of Four*

From his first recorded adventure, wherein he sniffs the lips of a dead man and detects the illusive whiff of poison, to the last adventure described in *The Case Book,* where his hawk-like nose captures the odour of gas beneath the tang of fresh paint, Mr. Holmes's olfactory abilities have served as a sterling example to the professional winetaster. The similarities between the detecting and tasting professions are, indeed, noteworthy as evidenced by a comparison of the following extracts from the canon with those from *The Taste of Wine* by Professor Émile Peynaud.

THE INDIVIDUAL

PEYNAUD
The winetaster must be coldly precise in his descriptive analysis, exacting in his approval but warm in his judgment.

HOLMES
Holmes had a cold, precise but admirably balanced mind.

* * *

PEYNAUD
As a winetaster you must be able to create a sensory void around yourself, excluding any superfluous sensations which might distract your attention.

HOLMES
I find that a concentrated atmosphere helps a concentration of thought. I have not pushed it to the length of getting into a box to think, but that is the logical outcome of my convictions.

* * *

PEYNAUD
Early childhood is fundamental to the development of our senses; and to develop well, each sense requires a proper introductory education and, later on, a more methodical training, for their performance can always be improved.

HOLMES
"Like all other arts, the Science of Deduction and Analysis is one which can only be acquired by long and patient study, nor is life long enough to allow any mortal to obtain the highest possible perfection."

PEYNAUD
It is difficult to decide to what extent sensitivity of taste is innate and to what extent it is acquired.

WATSON to HOLMES
"In your own case," said I, "from all you have told me, it seems obvious that your faculty of observation and your peculiar facility for deduction are due to your own systematic training"

"To some extent." he answered thoughtfully... "Art in the blood is liable to take the strangest forms... my brother Mycroft possesses it in a larger degree than I do."

TRAINING

PEYNAUD
The... analytic approach to tasting is based on logic and reasoning. It is knowledge gained by a step-by-step deductive process.

HOLMES
From long habit the train of thoughts ran so swiftly through my mind that I arrived at the conclusion without being conscious of intermediate steps. There were such steps, however.

* * *

PEYNAUD
Knowing and understanding an object, be it a face, an odour or a wine, is based on observation by one's senses; but a single, rapid encounter is inadequate for knowledge in depth. Thus one comes to understand wine by a thorough and detailed analysis of tastes and smells, and by noting down as many characteristics as possible.

HOLMES

My eyes have been trained to examine faces and not their trimmings. It is the first quality of a criminal investigator that he should see through the disguise.

* * *

PEYNAUD

The expert... seeks clarity and precision above all in his expression. His style is strict and economical but his comments are reasoned; his conciseness is not due to a lack of imagination but to a choice of the most precise words, and in his reports he only uses terms with an accepted and agreed meaning.

[The style of] the more occasional taster and the informed amateur... [is] more full of imagery but less precise.

WATSON to HOLMES

"Right in the middle of them, a little island of ancient culture and comfort, lies this old home, surrounded by a high sun-baked wall mottled with lichens and topped with moss, the sort of wall..."

"Cut out the poetry, Watson," said Holmes severely. "I note that it was a high brick wall."

* * *

PEYNAUD

Too often we eat, drink, and taste without paying any real attention to what we are tasting and smelling and in such cases we end up noticing practically nothing. Countless sensations pass unremarked...

HOLMES
You see but you do not observe. The distinction is clear. For example you have frequently seen the steps which lead up from the hall to this room... How many are there?

DEDUCTION

PEYNAUD
Suggestion and autosuggestion can both induce tasting errors and the taster must be able to resist them. He needs to be wary of his imagination too, a taste imagined or anticipated is already half perceived.

HOLMES
It is a capital mistake to theorize before you have all the evidence. It biases the judgment.

* * *

PEYNAUD
For anyone who has followed the winemaking of the past thirty or so harvests, identifying a vintage may seem somewhat easier; the process is one of reasoning, elimination and deduction. Knowing the annual weather cycles and consequent state of the grapes at vintage time will enable one to rule out certain vintages leaving just a few to choose from.

WATSON to HOLMES
"But I have heard all you have heard."
"Without, however, the knowledge of preexisting cases which serve me so well..."

PEYNAUD
As to identifying an individual vineyard or property, the wine needs to be one with a very distinctive personality. A wine without any personality gives one

no reference point by which to remember it, and if it has no family traits, no indications as to its origins it has little chance of being recognized or identified.

HOLMES
Singularity is almost invariably a clue. The more featureless and commonplace a crime is, the more difficult it is to bring it home.

* * *

PEYNAUD
When a taster has become accustomed to certain conditions, a regular tasting room, a particular shape of glass or tastevin, for example, then he may well be put off in different circumstances. For this reason tasting conditions should be as systematically organized as possible... In these circumstances his sensitivity is also at its most acute...

WATSON on HOLMES
He was a man of habits, narrow and concentrated habits, and I had become one of them. As an institution I was like the violin, the shag tobacco, the old black pipe, the index books, and other perhaps less excusable... I was a whetstone for his mind. I stimulated him. He liked to think aloud in my presence. His remarks could hardly be said to be made to me - many of them would have been as appropriately addressed to his bedstead - but none the less, having formed the habit, it had become in some way helpful that I should register and interject.

RESULTS

PEYNAUD
[Expert tasters'] tasting analyses probe deeper; they can explain a defect and pinpoint its source, trace a wine's past, predict its future.

HOLMES
The ideal reasoner would, when he has once been shown a single fact in all its bearing, deduce from it not only all the chain of events which led up to it, but also all the results which would follow it.

PEYNAUD
The taste image on your palate is compared with a host of images stored and classified in the mind . . .

HOLMES
The skilful workman is very careful indeed as to what he takes into his brain-attic. He will have nothing but the tools which may help him in doing his work, but of these he has a large assortment, and all in the most perfect order.

PEYNAUD
The taster who has learned how to interpret tastes and smells sizes up and appreciates a wine with a sniff and a taste in much the same way that the reader grasps the meaning of a book title, a phrase, or a sign instantly. He can 'read' a wine, whereas the layman unfamiliar with the taste alphabet finds such reading difficult.

HOLMES
"Elementary. It is one of those instances where the reasoner can produce an effect which seem remarkable to his audience, because the latter has missed the one little point which is the basis of the education."

BERNARD GINESTET quoted by PEYNAUD
In matters of winetasting there is no such thing as infallibility... all of us go through some periods that are better than others, during which we can be remarkably successful at identifying wines blind... I myself have experienced moments of glory where everything seemed obvious to me, and I have also drunk the cup of humility to the dregs when, unable to interpret any clue at all, I have ended up making enormous blunders. Winetasting is one of the finest schools for teaching modesty.

HOLMES
I made a blunder, my dear Watson - which is, I am afraid, a more common occurrence than anyone would think who only knows me through your memoirs.

HOLMES to WATSON
If it should ever strike you that I am getting a little overconfident in my powers, or giving less pains to a case than it deserve, kindly whisper 'Norbury' in my ear, and I shall be infinitely obliged to you.

PEYNAUD
From the length of [time between picking up a glass and the moment when the taste of the wine disappears after swallowing], which varies according to the drinker's preferences, and from the size of each mouthful of wine taken, one can tell, without [the drinker's] knowing, how discriminating a palate he has, even the extent of his general connoisseurship. Show me how you drink and I will tell you who you are.

MEDICINAL BREWS

SPRUCE BEER - For internal ailments, especially gastric ulcers.

Dissolve two pounds of black treacle, molasses or essence of malt into a gallon of warm water. Put it into a cask and add to it one gallon of cold water (spring water if available). Add to this mixture two tablespoonfuls of essence of spruce and, when the liquor is tepid, stir in a little good ale yeast. Leave the cask tightly covered in a warm place for a day or two, when fermentation stops, bung it firmly. It will be ready for use in a week.

GINGER BEER - Refreshing restorative

3 pounds of white sugar
1½ oz. cream of tartar
2 oz. of bruised ginger juice and rind of two lemons
3 gallons of boiling water
1 teaspoon sugar
1½ oz. yeast

Put sugar, cream of tartar, ginger and lemon juice and rind in a pan. Pour over three gallons of boiling water and stir until the sugar has dissolve and the liquor is cool. Take a little of the beer and dissolve in it the teaspoon of sugar and the yeast. Add this starter to the must and stir until it is well mixed. Cover the pan with a thick cloth and stand in a warm place for 24 hours. Skim off the yeasty cap and siphon off the beer from the sediment. Bottle in stone jars or strong beer bottles. Cork firmly. The beer will be ready in three days.

TONIC STOUT - A general panacea

8 oz. black or burnt malt
1 oz. hops
1 oz. dried stinging nettles
¼ oz. black liquorice
2 potatoes, cut into pieces
2 oz. brown sugar
1 oz. yeast
10 pints water

Bring the water to the boil. Then add it to the herbs, malt, hops, liquorice and potatoes. Simmer all gently together for an hour, then strain into a pan, add the sugar. Continue to simmer for an hour. Strain. Let it cool to blood-heat, then stir in the yeast. Cover the pan tightly and let it stand for 24 hours. Skim well, bottle and cork only lightly for another twelve hours. Then drive in the corks, leave for two days and the beer will be ready.

DANDELION WINE - Tonic

1 gallon dandelion flower petals
1 gallon boiling water orange
1 lemon
3 pounds of sugar
an inch of whole ginger well bruised
½ oz yeast on a slice of toast.

Wash the dandelion flowers, then cover them with boiling water. Let them stand three days, stirring often before squeezing the liquid from the flowers and straining into a pan. Add the thinly pared yellow zest from the lemon and orange, the sugar, the ginger and the sliced lemon and orange. Boil for 20 minutes. Let cool. Spread the yeast on the toast and float in the liquid. Ferment for 6 days then strain and bottle, corking loosely until all fermentation ceases.

ELDERBERRY WINE - a cathartic and astringent, specific against all bronchial troubles and a cold cure.

10 pounds elderberries
10 quarts of water
10 pounds of sugar
2 oz. ginger
2 bruised nutmegs
1 pinch cayenne pepper
Isinglass

Boil the elderberries in the water for three quarters of an hour. Strain and leave to cool. Add the sugar, ginger, cayenne pepper and a little isinglass dissolved in water for fining. Keep the wine in an earthenware vessel for the first few days. Fermentation will begin without the aid of yeast. After 14 days (or end of fermentation) it should be racked from the lees into a clean vessel, stoppered and set aside to mature. Bottle in six months.

CHERRY BOUNCE (Mrs. Beeton's version) - tonic

Stone twelve pounds of cherries, put them into a stone jar and set it on the stove in a pan of water until the juice runs freely. Strain the liquid from the pulp and add four pounds of sugar, a quarter of a teaspoon of allspice and four blades of mace to each gallon and bring to the boil again. Keep it simmering until all scum has disappeared from the surface of the juice. When it cools, add a quart of brandy and a quart of rum, stir well and bottle. It will be ready in three months.

HONEYED RHEUMATISM CURES

METHEGLIN

5 pounds (6¾ c.) Honey (lime blossom is especially good)
1 bunch of Thyme
1 bunch of Lemon Balm
1 bunch Rosemary
10 Cloves
6 crushed Allspice berries
1 Cinnamon stick
A piece of bruised Ginger root
1 Mace blade
5 pints wine yeast

Put 1¼ gallons of water in a large pan and simmer the herbs and spice in it for one hour. Strain warm onto the honey and stir. Allow it to cool, then add the yeast. Pour it into a clean jar and keep the surplus liquid in a bottle for topping up later. Leave it to ferment in a warm room, over a dish to catch the overflowing liquid. Add the reserve liquid when necessary. When the frothing has stopped, insert an airlock. When bubbles no longer appear put it in a cold place for 2 weeks, keeping well corked. Siphon off into a clean jar, cork tightly and seal with wax. Store for 6 months. Siphon off again and pour into bottles, which should be well corked and wired down. Store the bottles on their sides for at least 2 years.

MEAD

1 ounce dried Hops
4 pounds Honey (freshly extracted from comb)
2 gallons water
1 ounce yeast spread on a piece of toast

Pour the water over the honey and hops and heat for one hour. Then strain it into a pan and leave it to cool before adding the yeast. Take out the toast on the following morning, and stir the liquid well. Cover the pan with a clean cloth (muslin or cheesecloth) and leave it for 5 days. Strain and pour it into bottles, but do not cork securely until the bubbling has ceased. The mead should be left one year before using.
Newly made mead retains a slight honey flavour. After long aging it becomes 'fierce'. It will keep indefinitely.

CURE FOR THE STING OF A BEE Bruise the leaf of a poppy, and apply it to the affected part.

DOMESTIC SUBSTITUTES FOR FOREIGN FAVOURITES

A NOTE ON THE VERSATILITY OF ELDERBERRY WINE

In her book *Country Wines,* Mary Aylett declares that:
Much of the 'founder's port' and other allegedly fine wines in the colleges of our universities may well be nothing in the world but elderberry wine, bought in good faith from a famous nineteenth century wine merchant, in a university town. The ports, clarets and Bordeaux wines retailed by this infamous wretch were once celebrated through the city and quantities of them were sold to both dons and undergraduates. Only a few persons, and those business associates corrupted by the trade, wondered that he imported so little and yet sold so much, for his cellars seemed to partake of the virtues of the widow's cruse in copiousness. The man subsequently retired with a handsome fortune, and upon his deathbed imparted to his son the secret of his riches. The famous wines were all elderberry, their flavour and colour adapted with vinegar or brown sugar, according to the type of red wine in demand.

GOOSEBERRY CHAMPAGNE
This wine was so often sold as French Champagne that its making was assumed to be a preliminary to fraud.

1 gallon gooseberries
12 grape leaves
1 gallon cold water
4 pounds white sugar

Break up the berries with a mallet. Put them into a bowl with the vine leaves. Cover with water. Mash the fruit and stir occasionally. Leave 12 days and then squeeze every drop of moisture from the gooseberries and leaves before throwing them away. Strain the liquid and add the sugar. Stir until it is dissolved and put in a warm room to ferment. Leave 8 days, then skim and bottle.

It takes about two years of cellaring to attain its sparkle.

BRAMBLE CLARET

1 gallon brambles
1 quart sloes
1 gallon boiling water
4 pounds sugar
½ oz yeast
1 large slice of toast

Pour the boiling water over the brambles (blackberries). Leave six days, mashing the fruit each day. Squeeze all moisture out of the fruit and throw the pulp away. Add the sugar, sloes and the yeast which has been spread on toast. Stir and mash the sloes every day for a fortnight as it is fermenting then skim and run through three thicknesses of muslin before bottling. Keep 6 months.

PLUM PORT

Plum and Damson 'Port' was sold as The Real Thing well into the 20th century.

As Lord Pembroke delighted in telling his guests, "I can't answer for my Champagne and my claret as I only have the word of my wine merchant that it is good, but I can answer for my port. I made it myself."

4 pounds damsons
1 gallon boiling water
3 pounds sugar
1 oz. ale yeast
Brandy

Boil the sugar with one gallon of spring water, skimming well until it is clear and add four pounds of damsons or plums and continue stirring and skimming for half an hour. When it is bright, strain into a jar. When it cools, crumble in the yeast and let it work for three or four days. Strain it from the lees and rack into a clean cask. If not quite brilliant, add half an ounce of isinglass, dissolved in some of the liquor. Keep the cask well topped up. When it ceases to work, set aside to mature or rack into a clean jar. Add brandy. In two years it will be like port wine and can be kept for much longer.

SEVILLE ORANGE SHERRY

Sherry's popularity made its imitation one of the main objectives of the home brewer.

12 Oranges
1 Lemon
2 pounds of sugar
1 gallon boiling water
1 teaspoon of ale yeast

Peel the oranges and lemon carefully with a sharp knife to insure that the pith is removed as its addition in the must would result in undrinkably bitter wine. Squeeze out the juice into a basin with the sugar and pour the boiling water over it. Stir until all the sugar is dissolved, cover it and leave it for two or three days, stirring several times a day. Then strain all the juice into a cask. Take a little warm orange juice and water and put into it a teaspoon of ale yeast. When this starter is working well add it to the cask. Cork it lightly. Keep it topped up with orange juice and water until fermentation has ceased, and then bung it and leave in a cool place for at least six months, then it may be bottled off and drunk at once, although it will improve with keeping.

DAISY WHISKY

4 quarts of the small field daisy blossoms
1 gallon boiling water
1 pound wheat
1 pound large raisins
2 lemons
2 oranges
3½ pounds sugar
1 oz. yeast

Put the daisies in a bowl and cover with the boiling water. Stand until next day then squeeze out the daisies. Slice the oranges and lemons into the liquid and add the sugar and stir until it is dissolved. Leave until luke warm. Then add the chopped raisins, wheat and sprinkle with yeast on top. Leave it for 21 days to ferment. Then skim, strain and bottle. Keep six months to mature.

PARSLEY BRANDY

½ pound Parsley
1 gallon Water
3½ pounds Sugar
2 Oranges
2 Lemons
½ slice Toast
1 ounce bruised Ginger Raisins.

Wash the parsley and add it to thé water and boil for 30 minutes, then strain and throw away the parsley. Halve the oranges and lemons and put them in a bowl with the sugar and the ginger. Pour the boiling liquid on and stir until sugar is dissolved. When lukewarm add the yeast spread on toast. After 7 days skim and bottle. Put two large juicy raisins into each bottle.

BIBLIOGRAPHY

Acton, Bryan *and* Duncan, Peter: Making wines like those you buy (Andover, Amateur Winemaker Publications, 1976)

Adams, Leon D.: The wines of America (New York, McGraw-Hill Book Company, 1985)

Anderson, Nels: Desert Saints, the Mormon frontier in Utah (Chicago, University of Chicago Press)

Anglade, Pierre, *editor*: Vins et vignobles de France (Paris, Larousse, 1987)

Ashley, Maureen: Italian wines (London, Webster's International Publishers, 1990)

Amerine, Maynard A. *and* Singleton, Vernon L.: Wine (Berkley, University of California Press, 1977)

Aylett, Mary: Country wines (London, Odhams Press, 1953)

Basile, Nicola Dante: Il vino in Italia (Il Sole 24 Ore Libro)

Beeton, Isabella Mary: Cookery book (London, Ward, Lock)

Berry Bros. & Co: Tokay (London, Berry Bros., 1933)

Berry, Charles Walter: Viniana (London, Constable, 1929)

Beswick, Francis: Traditional British honey drinks (Loughborough, Heart of Albion Press, 1992)

Bickerdyke, John: The curiosities of ale & beer (Originally published London in 1889, reissued New York, Benjamin Blom, 1971)

Blackall, Simon *and* Foulkes, Chris: Quaffing quotes and wine facts (Sydney, Watermark Press, 1984)

Brander, Michael: The essential guide to Scotch whisky (Edinburgh, Canon Publishing, 1990)

Broadbent Michael: The great vintage wine book (London, Mitchell Beazley, 1980)

Croft-Cooke, Rupert: Wine and other drinks (London and Glasgow, William Collins, 1962)

Dickens, Cedric: Drinking with Dickens (Reading, Elvendon Press, 1983)

Dunlop, John: Artificial and compulsory drinking usage of the United Kingdom (London, Houlston & Patterson, 1868)

Drahota, Rudolf: Drahota's recipes: a treatise on the manufacture of liquors, syrups, cordials and bitters (Philadelphia, Aschenbach & Miller, 1885)

Faith, Nicholas: The Winemasters: the story behind the glory and the scandal of Bordeaux (New York, Harper & Row, 1978)

Fiorani, E. *and* Fedecostante, R: Vini Medicinali (Milan, Erboristeria Domani-Libri)

Fleming, Alice: Alcohol: The delightful poison (New York, Delacorte Press, 1975)

Francatelli, Charles Elme *[Late Maître d'Hôtel and Chief Cook to Her Gracious Majesty Queen Victoria]*: A plain cookery book for the working classes (Originally published 1861, London, reissued Whitstable, Pryor Publications, 1993)

Garland, Sarah: Cooking with herbs and spices (Reader's Digest Books,1979)

Hallgarten, Fritz: Wine scandal (London, Weidenfeld & Nicolson, 1986)

Hanson, Anthony: Burgundy (London, Faber, 1982)

Herzbern, Robert: The perfect Martini book (New York, Harcourt, Brace, Jovanovich, 1979)

Hunt, Peter, *editor*: Eating and drinking - an anthology for epicures (London, Ebury Press,1961)

Hutchinson, Peggy: Home-made wine secrets (London, W. Foulsham & Co)

Huxley, Leonard, *editor*: Elizabeth Barrett Browning: letters to her sister, 1846 - 1859 (London, John Murray)

Jackson, David *and* Schuster, Danny: Grape growing & wine making: a handbook for cool climates (Martinborough, New Zealand, Alister Taylor Publishing Ltd., 1981)

Jackson, Michael: La Nuova Guida Mondiale della Birra (Milan, Pubblistampa, 1988)

Johnson, Hugh: The world atlas of wine (London, Mitchell Beazley, 1971)

Johnson, Hugh: The story of wine (London, Mitchell Beazley, 1989)

Johnson, Hugh: Wine (London, Mitchell Beazley, 1971)

Lawrence, R. de Treville III, *editor*: Jefferson and wine (The Plains, Virginia, Vinifera Growers Association, 1989)

Lender, Mark *and* Martin, James: Drinking in America: a history (New York, Free Press, 1982)

McDowall, R.S.J.: The whiskies of Scotland (London, John Murray, 1967)

Marrison, L.W.: Wines and spirits (London, Pelican Books, 1957)

Moore, Patrick: Guide to comets (London, Lutterworth, 1977)

Morton, P.: A book of other wines than French (New York, Alfred A. Knopf, 1929)

Pallar, Phillippa: Consuming passions (London, Redwood Press, 1973)

Pastena, Bruno: Saper bere il vino (Palermo, Dharba Editrice, 1990)

Pellucci, Emanuele: Antinori; Vintners in Florence (Florence, Vallecchi, 1981)

Peynaud, Émile: Knowing and making wine (London, John Wiley, 1984)

Peynaud, Émile: The taste of wine (London, MacDonald, 1983)

Piccinardi, Antonio *and* Sassi, Gianni: Il Libro degli Spiriti (Milan, Mondadori, 1987)

Redding, Cyrus: A history and description of modern wines, 3rd edition (London, 1851)

Rice, Susan: A compound of Excelsior (Dubuque, Gasogene Press, 1991)

Robinson, Jancis: Vines, grapes and wine (London, Mitchell Beazley, 1986)

Rollins, Hyder Edward: The letters of John Keats 1814 - 1821, vol 2 (Cambridge, Mass, Harvard University Press, 1958)

Saintsbury, George: Notes on a cellar-book (First published London, 1920: reissued London, Macmillan, 1963)

Scott, J. M.: Vineyards of France (London, Theodore Brun, 1950)

Secheri, Giuseppe: Il Libro Completo del Vino (Istituto Geografico de Agostini)

Simon, André: Vintagewise (London, Michael Joseph, 1945)

Thomases, Daniel: "Il Palato di Christie's" in *L'etichetta*, no.47, Year 11, June, 1994.

Tibbott, S. Minwel: Welsh fare (Cardiff, National Museum of Wales, 1976)

Valnet, Dr. Jean: The practice of aromatherapy (Saffron Walden, The C. W. Daniel Company, 1980)

Vizetelly, Henry: Facts about Port & Madeira (A facsimile reprint of an 1880 first edition)

Vizetelly, Henry: Facts about Sherry (A facsimile reprint of an 1876 first edition)

Waites, Aline *and* Hunter, Robin: The illustrated Victorian songbook (London, Michael Joseph, 1984)
Walker, Michael: Cocktails international (London, Harper Collins, 1983)
Whitfield, W.C., *editor*: Just cocktails (Three Mountaineers, 1939)

Abbey Grange 6
Adams, Leon 66
Addington, Dr 109
Adler, Irene 80,90
Adlum, John 60,66
Ale 83,84,86,87
Allen, Warner 39
Alsace 16
Antinori 25
Armagnac 73
Armitage, James 49
Aylett, Mary 57,128
Barnes, Josiah 4
Bay, Dr 102
Beaune 11,29,41,98
Beer 87,88,106,112
Beeton, Isabella M 126
Beni Carlos 12
Berry, C W 7,18,34,39,41,44-46, 48,73,94,109
Berry, Francis 42
Berry Brothers & Rudd 18
Bickerdyke, John 84
Birch wine 106
Bishop 85,103
Bitters 89,90,91,108,111
Black Peter 5,69,77
Black velvet 90
Blackberry wine 106,112
Blake, Arthur ff 48
Bordeaux 10,11,24,95,96,98
Brackenstall, Eustace 6
Bramble claret 129
Brandy 73f,82,83,87-91,111-2
Brandy smash 89
Brandy punch 82
Broadbent, Michael 11,29,32-3,38- 43,48,50
Brolio 25
Brooks, Stephen 18
Browning, Robert 24
Bruce-Partington Plans 78
Burgundy 11,12,29,40f,98
Burnt brandy & peach 88
Caeac, Dr 102
Cameron, Charles 107
Cardboard Box 37
Case of Identity 93
Case Book of Sherlock Holmes 115

Catawba 60
Caudle 86
Chablis 10
Chamberland, Dr 102
Champagne 10,33,36,44f,59f,83, 90,91,98,99,108,113
Champagne cocktail 90,91
Cherry bounce 126
Chianti 23f
Cider 99
Claret 37f,56,83,93
Cocktails 79f
Cognac 73,82
Collins, John 91
Collins, Tom 91
Comet vintages 32,35f
Copper Beeches 5,97
Corton 29,30,40
Courmont, Dr 102
Creeping Man 37
Crême de menthe 99
Croft-Cooke, Rupert 98
Cunningham brothers 112
Curaçoa 78,83,89-91,99
da Vinci, Leonardo 24
Daisy whisky 131
Dandelion wine 126
Davis, John 48
Defoe, Daniel 31
Dickens, Cedric 48,85
Dickens, Charles 99
Dog's nose 88
Doran, Hatty 31,92
Douro Wine Co. 57
Drebber, Enoch 6,68
Druitt, Robert 18,20,110
Dunhill 89
Dunlop, John 108
Eccles, Scott 112
Edward VII 52,62,99,109
Elderberry wine 126,128
Elizabeth I 71
Eppes, Francis 31
Essencia 17
Fancy brandy 89
Fedecostante, Roberto 102
Ferrier, John 65
Feuerheerd, H L 62
Fiorani, Eracoli 102

Flaugerguse, Honoré 36
Flip 87
Ford, Richard 50
Forrester, J J 56,57
Four 80
French pousse cafe 89
Frescobaldi 25,26
Furmint 17
General 83
Gin 75,80,89,91,92
Ginestet, Bernard 123
Ginger beer 125
Gladstone, William E 18,51,109
Gloag, Matthew 111
Gloria Scott 49,50,55
Goethe, Johann 24
Gooseberry champagne 128
Grand Marnier 90
Graves 39
Guinness 88,90,107,112
Hair of the dog 92
Half & half 80
Hallgarten, Fritz 58
Hanson, Anthony 12
Harslevelu 17
Harvey's Bristol Cream 53
Hathersley, Victor 112
Haut-Brion 13,30,31,40
Hayes, Reuben 5
Healy, Maurice 40
Hermitage 12
His Last Bow 15,101
Holmes, Mycroft 117
Honey 92,101f,126f
Hope, Hilda Trelawney 6
Hope, Jefferson 6,75
Hopkins, Stanley 5
Hot Toddy 111
Hound of the Baskervilles 115
Hubinet, Mr 62
Hungerford Park 84
Hunter, Violet 97
Huxtable, Thorneycroft 112
Irish whiskey 70f
James, Oliver 112
Jefferson, Thomas 31
Jersey cocktail 90
Johnson, Hugh 17,20,31,53
Jones, Athelney 115

Kirwan, William 96
Köhler & Frohling 61
Kummel 99
Lafite 10,30,38,39
Lagard, Henry A 25
Latour 10,13,30
Lavalle, Jules 29
Leo X, Pope 19
Lestrade, Sholto 4
Leybourne, George 63
Locke, John 31
Longfellow, Henry W 60
Longworth, Nicholas 60
MacDonogh, Giles 16,77
McGinty, Jack 59
Madeira 14,33,34,56,82,98,100,111
Man with the Twisted Lip 75
Mantegazza, Paolo 26
Maraschino 90,92,99
Margaux 13,30
Marrison, L W 76
Marsupial bottles 14
Martinez cocktail 92
Martinique 77
Mead 102f,127
Medoc 12
Melas, Mr 112
Melville, Mr 96
Metheglin 103,126
Meunier, Dr 102
Michelangelo Buonarroti 24
Miquel, Dr 102
Monro, Mr 96
Montrachet 11,29,30,43
Morel, Dr 102
Morstan, Mary 15,23,25
Moulton, Francis Hay 34,50,92
Mouton 10
Murdock, Ian 112
Naegle, John C 67
Niebla 51
Nipozzano 26
Noble Bachelor 4,27,50
Old Tom cocktail 91
Oloroso sherry 20
Osbourne, Vincent 77
Osler, William 112
Parsley brandy 131
Patterson Brothers 71

Peabody punch 82
Pembroke, Lord 129
Pepys, Samuel 31
Perry 99
Peynaud, Émile 28,115f
Phelps, Percy 112
Pimm, James 84
Pimm's cup 84
Pinot Gris 15,17
Pitt, William 109
Plum port 129
Pomerol 30
Pommard 98
Pommery, Madam 62
Pontac, Arnaud de 31
Port 7,14,34,47f,50,55f,85,86,100
Port cup 83
Port wine negus 85
Porter 107
Priory School 5
Prohibition 71
Punches 82f,99
Raleigh, Walter 71
Rance, John 6,80
Ratafia 99
Redding, Cyrus 12
Reigate Puzzle 96
Rice, Susan 101
Riscasoli, Bettino 25
Rob Roy 90
Romanée-Conti 10,29,41
Rosé champagne 99
Rothschild, Phillipe de 10,13
Rucastle, Alice 5
Rufina 26
Rum 76,82
Ryder, James 112
St-Émilion 30,39
Saintsbury, George 34,44-5,47-8, 51-2,58,62,72,75,78,85,99,10
Saltire, Lord 5
Sauternes 17,21,32
Scandal in Bohemia 75,80
Schwendi, Lazare de 17
Scotch 70f,90,92
Second Stain 6
Seville orange sherry 130
Shandy gaff 87
Sherry 14,50f,56,84,89,100,112

Sherry cobbler 85
Sholto, Thaddeus 19f,23f
Shoscombe Old Place 4,5
Sign of Four 15,23,44,47,81,115
Simon, André 39-42,44-48,108
Small, Jonathan 81
Smith, Hyrum 67
Smith, Joseph 66,68
Snow, Edward H 68
Solitary Cyclist 4
Spruce beer 124
Stamford, Young 40,79
Starkie, Walter 20
Stock Broker's Clerk 32
Strangerson, Joseph 68
Study in Scarlet 6,40,75,79,80
Sutherland, Mary 95
Swift, Jonathan 31
Tewahiddle 87
Thomas, Jerry 92
Three Students 6
Thudichum, Dr 51
Tokay 11,15f,23,32,33,103,109
Toller, Mr. 5
Toller, Mrs 5,97,98
Tonic stout 125
Trevor, James 55,58
Trockenbeerenauslese 17
Valley of Fear 3,59,65,79
Vamberry, Mr 93
Vance, Alfred 63
Veiled Lodger 43
Vermouth 89,92
Victoria, Queen 106
Vizetelly, Henry 57
Von Bork, Herr 19
Von Herling, Baron 19
Westhouse & Marbank 95
Whiskey peg 81
Whisky 70f,89,99,111
Wilson, Rev. 49
Windibank, James 93-95
Windigate, Mr. 4
Wisteria Lodge 96
Yellow Face 96
Yellow muscat 17
Young, Brigham 65,67